StyleCity
ISTANBUL

StyleCity

ISTANBUL

With over 300 colour photographs and 7 maps

Contents

Street Wise

Style Traveller

Series concept and editor: Lucas Dietrich
Jacket and book design: Grade Design Consultants
Original design and map concept: The Senate
Maps: Peter Bull

Research and texts: Damla Kürklü and
Zeynep Yener
Specially commissioned photography by
Bahadir Tanriöver

The StyleCity series is a completely independent
guide.

Although every effort has been made to ensure that
the information in this book is as up-to-date and as
accurate as possible at the time of going to press,
some details are liable to change.

Any copy of this book issued by the publisher as a
paperback is sold subject to the condition that it shall
not by way of trade or otherwise be lent, resold, hired
out or otherwise circulated without the publisher's
prior consent in any form of binding or cover other
than that in which it is published and without a
similar condition including these words being
imposed on a subsequent purchaser.

First published in the United Kingdom in 2005 by
Thames & Hudson Ltd, 181A High Holborn,
London WC1V 7QX

www.thamesandhudson.com

British Library Cataloguing-in-Publication Data
A catalogue record for this book is available from the
British Library

ISBN 13: 978-0-500-21016-1
ISBN 10: 0-500-21016-0

Printed in China by C & C Offset Printing Co Ltd

How to Use This Guide

The book features two principal sections: **Street Wise** and **Style Traveller**.

Street Wise, which is arranged by neighbourhood, features areas that can be covered in a day (and night) on foot and includes a variety of locations – cafés, shops, restaurants, museums, performance spaces, bars – that capture local flavour or are lesser-known destinations.

The establishments in the **Style Traveller** section represent the city's best and most characteristic locations – 'worth a detour' – and feature hotels (**sleep**), restaurants (**eat**), cafés and bars (**drink**), boutiques and shops (**shop**) and getaways (**retreat**).

Each location is shown as a circled number on the relevant neighbourhood map, which is intended to provide a rough idea of location and proximity to major sights and landmarks rather than precise position. Locations in each neighbourhood are presented sequentially by map number. Each entry in the **Style Traveller** has two numbers: the top one refers to the page number of the neighbourhood map on which it appears; the second number is its location.

For example, the visitor might begin by selecting a hotel from the **Style Traveller** section. Upon arrival, **Street Wise** might lead him to the best joint for coffee before guiding him to a house-museum nearby. After lunch he might go to find a special jewelry store listed in the **shop** section. For a memorable dining experience, he might consult his neighbourhood section to find the nearest restaurant crossreferenced to **eat** in **Style Traveller**.

Street addresses are given in each entry, and complete information – including email and web addresses – is listed in the alphabetical **contact** section. Travel and contact details for the destinations in **retreat** are given at the end of **contact**.

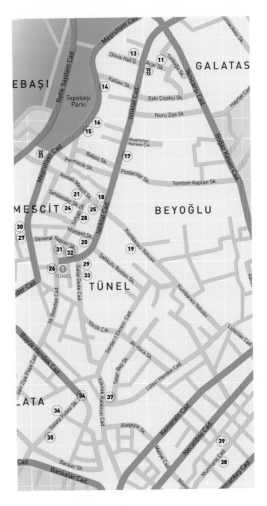

Legend

(2)	Location
■	Museums, sights
■	Gardens, squares
T M	Tünel and Metro stops
▦	Streets

ISTANBUL

As They Might Be Giants so catchingly put it, Istanbul (not Constantinople) is a bit of Turkish delight on a moonlit night. Few can fail to fall under the magical spell of its glorious location and breathtakingly beautiful buildings, all drenched with the irresistible allure of a thrillingly action-packed history. Confusingly possessing three different names at various times over the centuries (the first being Byzantium), Istanbul has the unique distinction of straddling two continents, Asia and Europe, yet refuses to be defined by either. The picture-postcard Bosphorus (Boğaziçi) separates the suburbs on the Asian shore from the city centre on the European side, itself further divided by the Golden Horn (Haliç). Geography and history have dictated the evolution of Istanbul's singular and complex character: East meets West here, and the Islamic past mingles with the modern Europe of today.

With bygone eras piled in archaeological layers one on top of the other, history oozes from the city's every pore. On the surface, designer shops and trendy cafés appear and vanish at the speed of light, but underneath another world of architectural splendour remains beautiful and timeless. But in the face of such contrasts, and despite recent decades of ambitious and unsympathetic city planning, Istanbul has somehow managed to hang on to its undeniable charm.

Originally one of several Greek colonies clustered around the shores of the Bosphorus and the Sea of Marmara (Marmara Denizi), Byzantium was already up and running by the middle of the 7th century BC, and was more than a thousand years old by the time Constantine the Great established the city (renamed Constantinople) as the capital of the Eastern Roman Empire in AD 330. Two hundred years later after a failed insurrection, the emperor Justinian, together with his infamous empress Theodora, set out to recreate a grander and more imposing city than ever before. The jewel in his municipal crown was the newly-built Hagia Sophia (dedicated in 537), which still stands as Istanbul's most distinctive monument. When the Byzantine Empire collapsed in 1453, Sultan Mehmet II (later known as Mehmet the Conqueror), with the help of a devoted army, quickly went to work to create the distinctively Ottoman Istanbul that underpins much of the modern city. The modern-day skyline over the Golden Horn, dominated by domes and minarets, is the fruit of this 15th-century vision.

In the the city's oldest quarter, Sultanahmet, the Muslim presence is unmistakable, with a mosque on every corner and calls to prayer ringing through the narrow streets. Within walking distance further along the Golden Horn, Istanbul's Christian Byzantine past can be found in the two urban neighbourhoods of Fener and Balat, which house the Greek 13th-century Panaghia Mouchliotissa (p. 46) and the Bulgarian 19th-century Bulgar Kilisesi (p. 44). The old port neighbourhood of Karaköy, located across the Golden Horn from Sultanahmet, has been an important trade centre since the days of the Ottoman Empire, and after a period of neglect is firmly back on the map with the opening of the city's premier museum of contemporary art, İstanbul Modern (p. 27). The pedestrian İstiklal Caddesi cuts a swathe north from Karaköy through the bohemian district of Beyoğlu, a large, indistinctly defined area that incorporates several neighbourhoods, including the trendy Cihangir and Çukurcuma, magnets for the city's young boho-chic shoppers.

Snaking north from Beyoğlu and the Sea of Marmara to join the Black Sea (Karadeniz), the Bosphorus is famed for both its strategic naval importance and for its jaw-droppingly picturesque atmosphere, beloved of visitors and filmmakers alike. Further up along its shores is Nişantaşı, the European face of Istanbul, and a fashion paradise since the 19th century. Nearby Ulus, containing Ulus Parkı, which itself houses Istanbul's most stunningly romantic restaurants, Ulus 29 (p. 143) and Sunset Grill & Bar (p. 88), is a recent addition to the city's commercial scene, developed during the past 20 years. Further still is the wealthy enclave of Levent and Etiler, home to corporate skyscrapers, fabulous restaurants, and equally fabulous villas just glimpsed behind their security walls. Across the Bosphorus from Beyoğlu and Sultanahmet are the two main neighbourhoods of the Asian side, Kadıköy, formerly the ancient Greek colony of Chalcedon and today the home of the Fenerbahçe football club, and Üsküdar, the site of Istanbul's largest concentration of mosques, built on the Asian shore thanks to its closer location to Mecca.

'Istanbul's fate is my fate', declares Orhan Pamuk in his recent memoir, a tribute to the city he has never left. Despite the continuing problems of pollution and a lack of green spaces, this metropolis of two continents, seven hills and twenty million people remains a city of contrasts and surprises that never fails to fascinate.

Street Wise

Taksim • Galatasaray • Beyoğlu • Tünel • Galata •
Karaköy • Old Istanbul • Çukurcuma • Cihangir • Harbiye •
Nişantaşı • Teşvikiye • Maçka • Levent • Etiler • Ulus •
The Bosphorus• Asian Side

Taksim
Galatasaray
Beyoğlu
Tünel
Galata
Karaköy

Taksim is, to paraphrase Frank Sinatra, the part of the city that doesn't sleep. During the day this hub of modern Istanbul is in a state of constant motion, with shoppers, officeworkers and museumgoers always on the move. When the sun goes down, the neon signs that line the bustling streets proclaim their wares and add a little modernity to a century-old setting.

Taksim Meydanı (Taksim Square) is dominated at its northern end by the Atatürk Kültür Merkezi (Atatürk Cultural Centre), the only purpose-built opera house in the city. Across from it is the İstiklal Anıtı (Independence Monument), commemorating the Turkish Republic's founder, Mustafa Kemal Atatürk, and which gives its name to the pedestrian avenue stretching behind it to Galatasaray. Formerly known as 'La Grande Rue de Pera,' İstiklal Caddesi is the main artery of Beyoğlu, the city's entertainment and culinary centre, and is an ideal place in which to indulge in a spot of people-watching.

Formerly called Pera, Beyoğlu was developed in the 19th century by European diplomats and merchants, who embarked on an ambitious building scheme and brought a fashionable European flair to the ancient Oriental city. Although the bygone splendour of old Pera is still apparent in the elegant Art Déco façades, the venues (and the dress-code) have been updated to reflect Beyoğlu's youthful, contemporary appeal. Çiçek Pasajı (Cite de Pera), formerly the home of some of Istanbul's most luxurious shops, is now occupied by a cluster of touristy meyhanes, but the architectural beauty of the arcade remains as a testament to the district's fading glamour. The 1990s saw a period of regeneration in Beyoğlu, and the old tram, which in its heyday carried its smart passengers from Taksim Square to Tünel, has been renovated and is back in service. Passage Markiz has, likewise, been revamped into a five-storey shopping complex, and houses Patisserie Markiz (p. 157), beloved of Pera's 19th-century literati, which has also been resurrected from the ashes.

At the terminus of the modern tram line and the point where İstiklal Caddesi comes to an end is Tünel (p. 22), the old underground transportation system which connects Beyoğlu to Karaköy and gives its name to the local area. Further down the peninsula towards the Golden Horn, Galata Kulesi (p. 24), the only surviving remnant from the 14th-century Genoese colony, rises to the sky. Further still, on the edge of the Golden Horn, is Karaköy, one of the oldest areas of settlement in Istanbul, and which today serves as an international port. As a foil to its ancient history, Karaköy now also houses İstanbul Modern (p. 27), the city's largest contemporary art museum, along with a chic café (p. 160).

Under the guidance of Ottoman art expert Serdar Gülgün, swanky department store Vakko offers a unique shopping experience in its second-floor home décor section. Taking inspiration from 16th- and 17th-century İznik tiles and Ottoman motifs, and realizing them with modern technology, Vakko has produced an elegant collection of soft furnishings, including cushions, throws, linens and tablecloths. There is also a special collection of porcelain manufactured by well-known Turkish brand Kütahya Porselen, using the Ottoman motif *Bihter* (Bill Clinton is said to be a fan). Recently, paintings by İsmail Acar have been added to the product range.

Trainers may be trendy and comfortable, but such unglamorous footwear has no place at Havai Lostra Salonu. Rather than a snooty club with strict dress codes, Havai Lostra is an old-fashioned shoe-shine, famous among city natives for the quality of its home-made shoe polish. With a décor that has not changed since the day it opened in 1951 (very kitsch and retro, with ocean-blue walls accompanied by orange faux-leather seats), Havai Lostra preserves the leisurely tradition of getting your shoes shined whilst comfortably enthroned, instead of doing it yourself at home.

4 Balık Pazarı + Nevizade Sokak

Sahne Sokak

This historic fish market and the adjacent narrow, cobbled Nevizade Sokak (a noisy street crowded with about thirty *meyhanes*) bustle with trade all day long. Be sure to visit Saraylar, which has served Istanbul's best and largest selection of cheeses and *meze* since the 1930s. Another worthy stop is Reşat Yazgüneş Balıkçısı, the oldest fishmonger in the market. Of the *meyhanes*, Boncuk specializes in Armenian cuisine, and İmroz is known for its delicious *meze*. During the summer months, the restaurants all bring tables out into the street (undeterred by its steep pitch), and the entire street becomes an open-air *meyhane*, accompanied by musicians wandering from table to table and copious glasses of *rakı*.

PROFITEROLE ANYONE?

5 İnci Pastanesi

İstiklal Caddesi 124/2

This is one of the few places in Istanbul that hasn't changed a bit since it opened in 1944. Still run by original owner Luca Zgonidis, who has been baking cakes since he was twelve, İnci Pastanesi is a true Beyoğlu institution and is famous for its gooey, chocolate-smothered profiteroles. İnci Pastanesi has a large and dedicated following, who clamour for the few tables available at which to sit and munch purchases. Along with the profiteroles, other 'sweets' on offer are quince paste and chicken-breast pudding.

FUSION INTRUSION

6 Changa

142

HIP TO BE AT THE SQUARE
7 Café Marmara
Taksim Meydanı

This French-style café on the ground floor of the Marmara Istanbul Hotel has been the meeting point of Istanbul's yuppies since 1993. With its location on the west side of Taksim Meydanı, right in the heart of the city, the café takes full advantage of its central location and is always bursting with noisily chatting customers. Serving meals all day long, the café's dessert and chocolate stand makes this place extra special, and afternoon tea is a delicious, if calorie-laden, treat. Café Marmara is a great place to watch the action in the square, if somewhat less so for the Monday morning diet.

ROYAL APPROVAL
8 Hacı Abdullah

RED OR WHITE?
9 Viktor Levi

VIEWS FROM ABOVE
10 360 İstanbul

GALLERY-LIKE CAFÉ
11 Kafe Ara
Tosbağa Sokak 8

Photography buffs know the name of Turkish photographer Ara Güler, and many think he is the owner of this nostalgically decorated café, as his work is displayed on the walls and the artist himself can be found most days sitting at his usual table, opening his post and reading art magazines. In fact, Güler is merely a neighbour, working from a studio in the next-door apartment building. Kafe Ara was founded by Yaşar Kartoğlu, a film director, with the intention of entertaining his movie friends. But the café's wallet-friendly prices and enormous portions have ensured that Kafe Ara has become hugely popular with Beyoğlu's in-crowd. The wait for a table might be longish, but the menu and the intellectual vibe are worth it.

ART OF COOL
12 Galerist
İstiklal Caddesi 311/4

Since its 2001 opening in Teşvikiye, one of Istanbul's wealthiest districts, Galerist has become a mecca for contemporary art fans. Chosen as one of the world's twelve most promising galleries by London's Royal College of Art, this young and innovative gallery represents such Turkish artists as Haluk Akakçe, Ergin Çavuşoğlu and Leyla Gediz, as well as fashion designer Hussein Chalayan. Attempting to break free from the problems that beset most Istanbul galleries – lack of space and lots of smoke – owner Murat Pilevneli moved Galerist in 2004 to its present premises in Beyoğlu's desirable 19th-century Mısır Apartmanı.

HAND-MADE HATS
13 Butik Katia
Danışman Geçidi 37´

Danışman Geçidi leads into a peaceful cobbled courtyard surrounded by old shops, one of which is particularly eye-catching in its old-fashioned charm. Madame Katia started her hat business during the more elegantly hat-friendly 1950s, with *chapeaux* brought back from various Parisian jaunts. Soon she began making her own creations, which were quickly snapped up by the wealthy ladies of Pera. Though there were several hat shops then, today only Butik Katia survives, and even its trade is mostly rental. But custom-made hats can still be ordered from Madame Katia's daughter, who runs the shop today.

MEET ME IN THE LOBBY
14 Grand Hotel de Londres
Meşrutiyet Caddesi 117

At the turn of the 20th century, Grand Hotel de Londres, built in 1892 and overlooking the Golden Horn, was one of the most prestigious temporary addresses in Pera, with its 54 beautifully decorated rooms and grand lobby. Unfortunately, the hotel has suffered somewhat due to management indifference, but don't let this rather sad state of affairs prevent you from visiting this bastion to faded bohemian elegance. Having coffee in the lobby is still a pleasant way to while away an afternoon, and a chance to catch a glimpse of the hotel's former grandeur. With its Victorian Ottoman style, Grand Hotel de Londres is a reminder, if a somewhat careworn one, of days gone by.

Istanbul has many English-language bookshops, and Robinson Crusoe, with its large stock and quality service, is one of the best. Behind the wood-and-glass façade, a library-like atmosphere encourages reading and (one assumes the owners hope) shopping. Founded in 1994 by Mehmet Güreli, Deniz Kunkut and Uğur Eruzun, Robinson Crusoe offers best-sellers and new releases, along with a wide variety of books on cinema, art and literature. Behind the cashier's desk is the largest selection of international glossies in town. Also on the shelves are travel guides and histories of Istanbul and Turkey.

Rather enterprisingly, Lokal, opened in 2001 by owner Sashah Khan, produces a riot of global cuisines (Indian, Thai, Vietnamese and Japanese, to name a few), tucked away in a quiet alleyway opening onto İstiklal Caddesi. The ultra-kitsch interior includes vivid green walls and an enormous poster of palm trees edged in light bulbs, with a large wooden table in the centre and smaller white lacquered ones scattered around it. While waiting for meals to arrive, diners can amuse themselves by watching chefs do their thing in the open-plan kitchen, or play with the robot toys thoughtfully placed at each table. Menus are tucked between old LP sleeves, and the bill arrives in a CD case. Reservations are strongly recommended for evenings. At lunch-time, Lokal serves reasonably priced set menus that attract the neighbourhood's ad agency crowd.

A LEGEND IN HIS OWN RESTAURANT

21 Yakup 2

159

ORIENTAL INTRIGUE

22 Pera Palas

136

SPIES LIKE US

23 Orient Bar

157

LIVE THE MUSIC

24 Babylon

Şehbender Sokak 3

Since opening its doors in 1999, Babylon has become the premier live music club in Istanbul, influencing the urban culture of the city and changing the fate of Beyoğlu's Tünel district. Following its success, countless variations on the café-restaurant-bar theme began springing up all over the neighbourhood, and soon the area was reborn as Istanbul's new centre of entertainment. Babylon's monthly programme has many loyal patrons who ensure that the place is always over-crowded. As well as hosting shows by music groups and DJs, the two-storey club also acts as a performance space and gallery.

ŞİMDİ MEANS NOW

25 Şimdi

Asmalı Mescit Sokak 8

Şimdi, owned by Aydın Kandemir and Alp Ekşioğlu, is housed on the ground floor of a beautiful 1902 Beyoğlu apartment building. Just like the building it is located in, the café, whose name means 'now' in Turkish, boasts history within its airy premises. Even the coffee machine, a Faema model E61, the first-ever coffee machine to use a pump, is historic. The mismatched décor includes an olive-green velvet-upholstered armchair, which in its former life was a wedding gift from Kandemir's grandmother to her daughter-in-law. But the real beauty lies at the rear of the café, which occupies the building's inner courtyard. Just raise your head above, and you'll see what we mean.

26 Tünel

Tünel Meydanı

The little square at the end of the pedestrian İstiklal Caddesi takes its name from this, Europe's first and shortest underground system. Built by French engineer Henry Gavan in the late 19th century, at the request of Sultan Abdülaziz and with a loan from the English government, construction was finished in three years. Initially used to transport animals, the two carriages soon began to ferry European diplomats and businessmen from their waterside offices in Karaköy to their hilltop residences in Pera. Today the original wooden cars have been replaced by modern metal ones, but this mini-underground ride (only 573 metres – and one minute – long) is still a great experience.

THAI ME ANOTHER

27 Pera Thai

Meşrutiyet Caddesi 134

The menu prices might frighten you off, but when it comes to Far Eastern fare, this restaurant is one of Istanbul's best. Housed in an elegant 19th-century building, Pera Thai rejoices in a refreshingly minimalist décor that eschews the more usual ethnic overload. The original Art

Nouveau ceiling frescoes provide the interior's only flamboyant touch, and threaten to divert diners' attention away from their dim sum. The menu offers such regional spicy specialities as crispy pork with garlic and chilli, steamed rice with coconut milk, and shrimp on toast. If you can stand the heat (and the hot plates), Pera Thai is definitely your place.

STREET OF TAVERNS

28 Sofyalı Sokak

- Refik, no. 7
- Sofyalı, no. 9
- Rakıcı, no. 5/1

Because of its proximity to bohemian Karaköy, Asmalımescit has always been a centre for artists and writers. Since the day it opened in 1954, Refik, a *meyhane* owned by the gregarious Refik Arslan, has hosted a self-consciously intellectual crowd. By contrast, Refik's neighbour Sofyalı, is livelier and full of Beyoğlu's young, thanks to its reasonable prices. This Greek-meets-Turkish restaurant, whose five storeys are connected by a narrow steel staircase that becomes astonishingly difficult to navigate after a few glasses of *rakı*, offers around twenty-five types of *meze*, accompanied by hot appetizers (*sofyalı börek* and *pazı sarma* are favourites). New kid on the block is Rakıcı, housed in a modern house with an ornate ceiling, which seems set to become the best-loved of them all. Even Refik Arslan has been seen eating here.

MUSIC BOUTIQUE

29 Lale Plak

Galip Dede Caddesi 1

Fifty years ago, brothers İbrahim and Yusuf Atala set up their music shop in Tünel Meydanı. Today run by Hakan Atala (the son of one of the founders), the shop still has a long list of regulars, searching out hard-to-find records. Lale Plak's stock focuses on jazz, ethnic and classical music, and its shelves are organized by type, country of origin, period and instrument. Atala knows his customers and musical tastes so well that he keeps track of CDs bought and opportunities missed (to be rectified at a later visit). Refreshingly, Lale Plak's well-informed staff is cheerfully generous with both knowledge and assistance.

WATCH THE BOYS GO BY

32 Kaffeehaus

Tünel Meydanı 4

As author Alfred Polgar observed, coffee houses are the best places in which to be alone in a crowded setting. The same is true at this two-storey lounge overlooking tiny Tünel Meydanı. Days start early at Kaffehaus, and its bagel-like *simits* are a favourite breakfast-on-the-run for nearby officeworkers. For lunch, Kaffeehaus offers daily specials, along with a permanent menu of salads and grills. The hotly coveted table by the window is brilliant for people-watching while reading your newspaper and sipping a latte. A large marble staircase leads to further seating upstairs. However, if you are allergic to cats, be warned that Kaffeehaus's resident feline is fond of sharing both your lap and your lunch.

WHIRLING DERVISHES

33 Galata Mevlevihanesi

Galip Dede Caddesi 15

Galata Mevlevihanesi (Mevlevi Whirling Hall) attracts hordes of tourists who gather here at 3 p.m. every weekend afternoon for the Sema ceremonies. Watching the dervish, with his headdress and white skirt (respectively symbolizing the ego's tombstone and shroud) on his journey to spiritual maturity is a dazzling experience. Built in 1491, the original *tekke* (dervish lodge) burned down in 1765, and the present lodge is a replica. The graveyard with its ornate tombstones contains the remains of the *şeyh* (leader) of the Mevlevihane, Galip Dede, and İbrahim Mütefferika, the founder of the first Arabic-Ottoman printing press in the 18th century.

GOT WINGS?

34 Galata Kulesi

Galata Kulesi Sokak

Built by Genoese colonists in the 14th century and rising some 60 metres above the Golden Horn, Galata Tower is the city's most prominent landmark. In 1638, Hezarfen Ahmed Çelebi, in one of his many attempts to fly, strapped on a pair of artificial wings and glided his way from the top of the tower to the Asian shore, thus making him the first man in history to fly and the tower very famous indeed. Although the upper floors house a very touristy restaurant and nightclub, it is worth venturing upstairs for the panoramic views of the Golden Horn, Sultanahmet and the Bosphorus. Huffing and puffing up the spiral stone staircase's 307 steps is no longer necessary as a lift was installed in 1997.

JAIL HOUSE BORSCHT

35 Galata Evi

Galata Kulesi Sokak 61

In its former life Galata Evi's premises served as the British Empire's civil prison between 1904 and 1919, and later as a British military police station. After changing hands several times, and functioning as a residence, office and metalwork atelier, the building was sold in 1991 to architects Nadire and Mete Göktuğ. The duo duly converted the building into a restaurant offering Georgian and Russian fare, while preserving the two commissarial rooms on the ground floor and the prison wards above. The addition of lots of wooden furniture gives the rooms a somewhat cosier feel than they once had. The menu starts with Russian *borscht*, followed by *ostri* (veal goulash with pepper, tomato, mushroom and coriander) or *pilmeni* (potato-filled ravioli), and finishes rather unexpectedly with tiramisu. Galata Evi is well worth visiting for the unusual character of both its menu and its history.

JAZZY MOMENTS

36 Nardis Jazz Club

Kuledibi Sokak 14

There aren't many live jazz clubs in Istanbul, so Nardis, located in a steep narrow street near the Galata Tower, is a particular, if hidden, gem. The club hosts classic, modern, fusion and ethnic jazz concerts within its barely-furnished premises. Marcus Miller, Massimo Marko, and some of the more well-known Turkish performers, such as İlhan Erşahin and Kerem Görsev, have all performed here. Though it is the music that draws the crowds, Nardis also offers a menu of bar snacks, pasta, salads and mixed grills. Whether you are looking for food for the soul or for the stomach, Nardis is an experience to savour.

37 Autoban
Tatar Bey Sokak 1/2

Having designed interiors for restaurants and bars all over Istanbul (including some featured in this book), architect Seyhan Özdemir and interior designer Sefer Çağlar set up Autoban in 2003. Located in their second-floor studio in Galata overlooking the Golden Horn, Autoban specializes in furniture and lighting design, with an emphasis on natural materials and local production techniques. The duo have recently caught the eye of the international press, and in January 2005 were nominated by design magazine *Wallpaper** as Young Designer of the Year.

ONLY FOR LUNCH
38 İstiridye Balık Lokantası
Mumhane Caddesi 94

Open only for lunch on weekdays, İstiridye Balık Lokantası is an artisan seafood eatery so beloved for its fish soup that it has become a favourite address of businessmen more accustomed to five-star dining. After serving for more than a decade in Perşembe Pazarı, İstiridye moved to its present location in 1985. The décor is simple, with wooden floors and black and white photographs of old Istanbul hanging on the walls. Apart from the fish soup, the menu offers a variety of seasonal fish, including the best paper-wrapped sea bass in Istanbul.

UP ON THE ROOF
39 Aya Andrea
Mumhane Caddesi 103

Just across the road from İstridye Balık Lokantası is a spectacular five-storey apartment building, an architectural beauty used by the Russians prior to World War I as a base on their way to Jerusalem. What makes the building even more special is the rooftop Aya Andrea chapel, a small Russian Orthodox church whose green cupola can just be seen from street level. Two other rooftop churches (Aya Panteleymon and Aya İlya) are also in the area. Aya Andrea is only open to the public on Sundays, but Aya Panteleymon and Aya İlya can be visited on any day, with permission from the caretakers of the apartment buildings.

STICKY FINGERS
40 Karaköy Güllüoğlu Baklavacısı
Mumhane Caddesi 171

Although the exact origin of baklava is unknown, Karaköy Güllüoğlu is a name that has become synonymous with it. Founded by Güllü Çelebi in Gaziantep in 1871, Karaköy Güllüoğlu moved to Istanbul in 1949, a time when the dessert was still fairly exotic. After months of giving it away free, interest began to pick up and soon the company was enlarging both its premises and product range (today there is even a diet version). Remaining faithful to traditional techniques while embracing the latest technology is, the owners claim, the key to Karaköy Güllüoğlu's success. Today the world's first baklava-producing factory churns out three tonnes of the stuff per day, exporting it to countries around the world. There are two shops on Mumhane Caddesi: one within the factory, and the other located under a parking garage. Both are primarily takeaway venues, although there are a few tables to sit at. House specialities include both the plain version and *sütlü nuriye*, made with sterilized milk.

MUSEUM WITH A VIEW
41 İstanbul Modern
Meclis-i Mebusan Caddesi Antrepo 4

An old warehouse on the Karaköy pier is now the site of the city's first contemporary art museum, which opened in 2004. Behind this long-standing venture is the Eczacıbaşı Group, which provided both the initial investment and the core collection. The museum covers 8,000 square metres and two floors connected by a glass and steel staircase, an installation designed by Monica Bonvicini for the 2003 Istanbul Biennial. The collection consists of works by contemporary Turkish artists, and at the moment is still owned by the Eczacıbaşı family. The entrance foyer houses an auditorium, a photography and video art gallery, and a new media centre. A sculpture garden is planned to adorn the entrance in the near future. The museum, curated by Rosa Martinez (curator of the Venice and Moscow biennials), also houses a shop and the chic and stylish İstanbul Modern Café (p. 160).

CAFÉ IN THE MUSEUM
42 İstanbul Modern Café
160

Old Istanbul

The centre of power in Istanbul since the Byzantine era, Sultanahmet is at the top of every visitor's must-see list. Taking its name from the boy king, Sultan Ahmet, who inherited an empire at the age of fourteen, this historic quarter with its familiar picture-postcard views has been the starting point for generations of sightseeing tours. Although it is often overcrowded with tourists, Sultanahmet's splendid remains of an empire are reason enough for a visit to this part of the city.

Aya Sofya (Hagia Sophia), once described as the greatest church in Christendom, is certainly one of the main attractions. Said to have been built by Constantine the Great in 325 on the remains of a pagan temple, the church was burnt to the ground and rebuilt by Justinian and Theodora two hundred years later. In 1453, Mehmet the Conqueror added minarets to the huge, soaring dome and turned the former church into a mosque. The building controversially became a museum in 1935, but the interior retains its religious associations with the Christian mosaics and Muslim calligraphic disks adorning its walls and piers.

Nearby is the Topkapı Sarayı (Topkapı Palace), home to the Ottoman sultans for three hundred years, and Sultanahmet Camii (Blue Mosque), built by Sultan Ahmet to rival Aya Sofya. Sultanahmet Camii's interior contains over 20,000 İznik tiles, whose bluish tint give the Blue Mosque its popular name. Alongside is the Hippodrome, a public park used in the days of the Byzantine empire for ceremonies and sporting events, and is now, as it was then, home to various spoils of empire, including the Egyptian obelisk (1,500 BC), the Serpentine Column (480 BC), and with its 4th-century date, the comparatively modern Column of Constantine. Venturing away from the sightseeing riches of Sultanahmet towards the shores of the Golden Horn — surely the most beautiful natural harbour in the world — are two bustling trade markets: the infamous Kapalıçarşı (Grand Bazaar), stuffed to overflowing with 300 shops and thousands of traders, shoppers and tourists, and the exotically pungent Mısır Çarşısı (Spice Bazaar; p. 167).

With the wails of muezzins echoing across the water and Süleymaniye Camii casting its enormous shadow, the character of Sultanahmet is firmly Islamic. Further along the coastal route are the districts of Fener and Balat, two charming, quiet neighbourhoods of historic and cultural importance. After the fall of Constantinople, Greeks, Jews and Italians established communities here, and the narrow, crooked streets are filled with churches and synagogues instead of mosques. Though suffering from neglect, this historic corner of Istanbul puts visitors in touch with its ancient and glorious past.

AUTHENTICALLY HISTORIC
1 Safa Meyhanesi

158

MOSQUE OF INSPIRATION
2 Küçük Ayasofya Camii
Küçük Ayasofya Caddesi

Commissioned by Justinian and Theodora in 527 (five years before they turned their attentions to Hagia Sophia), this former church dedicated to Sergius and Bacchus, patron saints of Christian soldiers in the Roman army, was converted into a mosque in the 16th century. Later called Küçük Ayasofya (Little Hagia Sophia) because of its resemblance to its more famous neighbour, the mosque is Istanbul's oldest surviving Byzantine monument still in use as a place of worship. Küçük Ayasofya's octagonal structure has been the inspiration for many mosques built in the ensuing years, including Hagia Sophia. Earthquakes and vibrations from the nearby railway have taken their toll, but a recent restoration programme is attempting to shore up the damage.

MINIATURE SÜLEYMANIYE
3 Sokullu Mehmet Paşa Camii
Şehit Mehmet Paşa Sokak 20

Built in 1571 on the site of an ancient church, this tiny mosque, along with so many others in the city, was designed by Mimar Sinan. Perched in a steep street, it is often overlooked by tourists thronging the more popular destinations of Sultanahmet. Its courtyard served as a *medrese* (seminary), surrounded by rooms used by scholars. It is worth venturing beyond the ever-present scaffolding as the interior is truly beautiful. The colour aquamarine dominates the İznik tiles adorning the pulpit and the *mihrab* and forming a frieze of floral motifs below the galleries, and is reflected in the carpets, creating a soothing and harmonious atmosphere.

DON'T INTERFERE!
4 Karışma Sen
Kennedy Caddesi 30

Rather than the name of the owner or a reflection of the menu, the unusual name of this hundred-year-old fish restaurant is a phrase that translates as 'don't interfere!' The story is that the restaurant functioned for years without a name, resulting in heated arguments over the years about what it should be called. 'Karışma sen' became a catchphrase muttered by locals and customers alike to prevent discussions getting out of hand. Eventually the name stuck, and has remained ever since. But Karışma Sen has another interesting history. During the Turkish war for independence, weaponry stolen from the Topkapı Sarayı was transferred to the Asian coast from the restaurant, and the famous puppet show, *Karagöz and Hacivat*, took place for the first time on the site of its premises.

CRETAN CREATION
5 Giritli
Keresteci Hakkı Sokak

Ayşe Şensılay, owner and chef of Giritli (*Girit* is Turkish for Crete), has drawn on her Cretan heritage to create a most unusual menu, pointing out that centuries of invasions and intermingling of cultures has produced an adaptable and resourceful cuisine. Such resourcefulness can be experienced at her two-storey restaurant, occupying a 19th-century Sultanahmet mansion next to the Armada Hotel. Served as a fixed menu (no exceptions), options include cold herb-based *meze* and hot appetizers such as octopus leg, together with seasonal fish dishes. *Börek* stuffed with apple and flavoured with cinnamon finishes off the meal. In the summer months, seating is available in the hotel's garden.

THE FISHER KING
6 Balıkçı Sabahattin

141

FAIRY TILES
7 Büyük Saray Mozaikleri Müzesi
Torun Sokağı

The Byzantine emperor Constantine caused something of a property boom when he built his residence, Palatium Magnum (Great Palace), on this Sultanahmet hilltop. Other Byzantine monuments followed, including Hagia Sophia, and after conquering the city, the Ottomans followed suit and settled on the same hill. The Great Palace Mosaic Museum, which houses the largest collection of 6th-century mosaics in the world, is in fact the remains of the courtyard of the Great Palace, unearthed in the 1950s by British and Austrian archaeologists. The courtyard's surviving ornamental pavement depicts hunting and mythological scenes. Today located in the shadow of Sultanahmet Camii, the museum offers a magical journey into ancient times.

8 Türk ve İslam Eserleri Müzesi

Atmeydanı Sokağı 46

The Museum of Turkish and Islamic Art was initially built in 1913 within one of Sinan's masterpieces, the Süleymaniye Camii's *külliye* (now housing Darüzziyafe, see p. 144), before moving to its present location in the İbrahim Paşa palace in 1983. One of the most impressive examples of 16th-century Ottoman architecture, the palace was a gift from Sultan Süleyman to his chief advisor, İbrahim Paşa, and is the only civilian palace in Istanbul to have survived into the present day. The museum has a collection of more than 40,000 works of Islamic art, including the largest rug collection in the world. Of particular interest is the Etnografya Müzesi, a natural history section incorporated within the larger museum that exhibits objects from the day-to-day existence of Turkey's historic peoples, including the Yürüks, a nomadic tribe of Anatolia.

9 Soğukçeşme Sokak

- Ayasofya Pansiyonları
- Konuk Evi
- Sarnıç Restaurant

Sandwiched between Hagia Sophia and Topkapı Sarayı, Soğukçeşme Sokak was an aging cobbled street in the shadows of the great mosque until 1986, when Çelik Gülersoy, head of the Turkish Touring and Automobile Association, stepped in. Years of restoration have swept away the crumbling mansions, and now a row of nine wooden houses operates as a pensione (Ayasofya Pansiyonları), offering Ottoman-style hospitality to its guests. Konuk Evi (Guest House), on the opposite side of the street, has a beautiful garden in which to sit on sunny summer days. A 1,600-year-old Roman cistern has been converted into the elegant Sarnıç Restaurant, illuminated by large candlelit chandeliers. Opinions differ as to how sympathetic or beneficial the restoration project has been.

16TH-CENTURY SPA

10 Çemberlitaş Hamamı

Vezirhanı Caddesi 8

This *hamam*, located in the midst of Istanbul's greatest monuments and in continual use since 1584, is an architectural treasure in itself, and remains a focal point for historians, photographers and filmmakers today. The architect (possibly Sinan, although this is open to debate) installed a natural floor heating system by inserting pipes into the marble blocks, allowing steam to travel through them and warm the platform. Unfortunately, the heating system, as well as the women's bath facility, was damaged during a less than successful renovation in 1972. The present owner, Ruşen Baltacı, is determined to transform the *hamam* into a modern spa without damaging its historical integrity. The present restoration, which has resulted in the partial closure of the *hamam*, is not due for completion until 2008.

TRUE BLUE GOLD

11 Kalsedon Maden İşletmeleri

Caferiye Sokak 2

Chalcedony, a blue semi-precious stone that has been in use since 800 BC, is believed to have metabolic and psychological properties. The largest reserve of the stone, often referred to as 'blue gold', is located in Eskişehir, in Central Anatolia. Sırrı and Birsen Gerçin, a husband-and-wife team, are the owners of the mine and of this elegant store-cum-gallery located in the shadow of Hagia Sophia. The 500-year-old building, once home to Fatih the Conqueror's teacher (Sırrı Gerçin is a descendant of the same teacher), now showcases jewelry and decorative accessories made from chalcedony.

HEART OF THE CITY
12 İbrahim Paşa Hotel

134

A PLACE TO PAUSE IN TIME
13 İstanbul Arkeoloji Müzeleri
Osman Hamdi Bey Yokuşu

İstanbul Arkeoloji Müzeleri, founded in the mid-19th century, is home to a world-class collection of archaeological artefacts. Located in the grounds of the Topkapı Sarayı, the museum's main building was designed by Alexander Vallaury, who took his inspiration from the Alexander Sarcophagus (exhibited inside), and is one of the best examples of neoclassical architecture in the city. With its rich collection of Hellenistic, Roman and Byzantine sculpture, as well as sarcophagi from the royal necropoli of Sidan, it is the main attraction of the entire complex. In the museum's courtyard, the Çinili Köşk (Tiled Pavilion), dating to 1472, is one of the oldest examples of civilian Ottoman architecture, and showcases the museum's collection of Seljukian and Ottoman tiles. Behind the main building is the Museum of the Ancient Orient, containing pre-Islamic objects from the Arabian Peninsula. The beautiful garden alone, with its historic graveyard, is worth a visit.

HISTORIC BATH & BAR
14 Cağaloğlu Hamamı
Kazım İsmail Gürkan Caddesi 34

Tracing their heritage back to the Romans, *hamams* were used as communal baths in ancient times. After many centuries and a great deal of improvement in domestic plumbing, they remain a social institution and one of life's greatest pleasures. Cağaloğlu Hamamı is located in Istanbul's historic district, near Hagia Sophia and the Grand Bazaar. A gift to the city from Sultan Mahmut I, it has been in operation since 1741, and as such is Turkey's first established company. Historic personages (including Edward VII and Florence Nightingale) and celebrities have all been here for a little indulgent pampering. Wear your *pestemal* (a thin, fringed bath towel) and *takunya* (wooden clogs), and once clean and serene, head to the Old Marble Bar (Cağaloğlu is the only *hamam* that serves alcohol). Almost as popular as the *hamam* itself, the bar is a favourite place among the locals, who gather here for an evening chat in a magical environment.

Istanbul owes a great deal of its present look to two foreign 19th-century architects, Alexander Vallaury and August Jachmund. Both men helped to establish the Ottoman Revival (also called Oriental Gothic), merging elements of classical Ottoman architecture with the European neoclassical style. Even if you aren't catching a train, the Sirkeci train station, designed by Jachmund, is worth a visit. Once the final terminal of the Orient Express, the station no longer serves international destinations, functioning instead as a suburban commuter hub. The Orient Express restaurant is beside the platform, but hungry travellers should venture across the road to Konyalı, a Turkish takeaway institution, for their deliciously savoury *böreks*.

As historic as the district it is located in, the confectionery Ali Muhiddin Hacı Bekir offers traditional Turkish sweets in suitably traditional style. Although today five different branches are scattered throughout the city, the original store (founded in 1777) remains quite unchanged. Around twenty varieties of Turkish delight and fifteen kinds of *akide şekeri* (boiled sweets) are stored in large glass jars, presenting a colourful, mouth-watering display. Halva, baklava and marzipan are packaged in boxes that feature a painting of the founder, Hacı Bekir, by the Italian artist, Preziosi (the original painting is in the Louvre). Hacı Bekir is a must for every tourist (and native) who wants a little taste of Turkish delights.

The number of staff employed at Hamdi Et Lokantası (there are over a hundred) should give you some idea of the fame of this restaurant, which attracts legions of local and international diners and churns out thousands of plates every day. After outgrowing its original venue, Hamdi Et Lokantası moved to this five-storey building next to Mısır Çarşısı in 1990. The first floor is reserved for VIP seating, whereas the fifth floor opens onto a terrace overlooking the Golden Horn. Originally from Urfa in Anatolia, owner Hamdi Arpacı concentrates on southeastern fare. On Fridays, the dish of the day is *döner* with pistachio, and *testi kebabı* (a meat dish cooked in earthenware jugs for about two hours) is served all week long.

This modest establishment has been trading in quality fur and leather goods since the 1960s, and such is its reputation that even the General Secretary of NATO took time from his presumably busy schedule to pay the shop a visit. Many of the world's best-known labels, including Giorgio Armani, Gianfranco Ferre and Dolce & Gabbana, send their designs here to be manufactured by Koç Deri. A luxurious array of furs are upstairs, whereas on the ground floor beautifully designed leather goods await both you and your wallet.

ORIENTAL DELICACY

25 Fes Café

Halıcılar Çarşısı Caddesi 62

A café within the Grand Bazaar may sound unpleasantly touristy, but such is not the case with Fes Café. Set into a cavernous niche with Philippe Starck-designed chairs, the vibe is more boho than so-so. Metin Tosun opened Fes in 1998, at a time when the bazaar was suffering from a lack of both locals and a decent place to eat, and soon found himself surrounded by competitors. Filled with tired shoppers stopping for coffee and carrot cake throughout the day, the café also draws locals who brave the bazaar just to pass the time at Fes.

TAKEAWAY HAMAM

26 Abdulla + Hamam

Halıcılar Çarşısı Caddesi 53

For a little piece of *hamam* pleasure in the comfort of your own home, visit Abdulla and Hamam, two shops facing one another on Halıcılar Caddesi, in the Grand Bazaar. Owner Metin Tosun, the man behind Fes Café (see this page), opened Abdulla and Hamam in 2001. Traditional crafts, including olive oil soaps, luxury towels, mohair blankets, sheepskin covers and *pestemals*, are sourced from all over Anatolia. Beaded curtains have recently been added to the répertoire, and visitors can chat with Mr Tosun while he is busily beading them.

CARPET MARKET
27 Adnan & Hasan

Halıcılar Çarşısı Caddesi 89–90–92

The Grand Bazaar, with over 300 shops and sky-high prices, is well known as the ultimate must-visit (but not necessarily must-buy) tourist destination. But the carpet and *kilim* shop Adnan & Hasan bucks the trend. Founded in 1978 and located in Halıcılar Çarşısı (which translates literally as 'the street of carpet-sellers'), Adnan & Hasan is run by Hasan Basri Semerci, who sources his gorgeous textiles from all over the country and is passionate and knowledgeable about each piece. Both antique and modern carpets are sold here, and all are hand-made. Best of all, Adnan & Hasan ships worldwide.

ORIGINAL HUBBLY BUBBLY
28 Erenler Nargile

Çorlulu Ali Paşa Medresesi 36/28

A centuries-old tradition, the smoking of the *nargile* (waterpipe) is still kept alive in a few coffee houses, most of them located in Tophane, Beyazıt and Aksaray. Among these is Erenler Nargile, one of the oldest and most famous *nargile* houses in Istanbul. Located in an historic Ottoman seminary in Beyazıt, Erenler is in a leafy courtyard surrounded by Ottoman-style couches and glass cupboards, showcasing different types of *nargile*. Playing host to a number of political and literary luminaries over the years, it has become a guidebook fixture. Visitors can either have a leisurely smoke, or buy a *nargile* to take back home. For the non-smoker, Erenler also offers tea and Turkish coffee.

THE CRAZY LADY

29 Deli Kızın Yeri

Halıcılar Çarşısı Caddesi 42

Calling herself 'the crazy lady' (*deli kız*), American Linda Caldwell has created a thriving business reinterpreting Anatolian handicrafts. Establishing an atelier in Arnavutköy in 1998, Caldwell began designing hand-made accessories as a hobby. Three years later, having run out of people to give her creations to as gifts, she set up shop in the Grand Bazaar. Her collection of place mats, tablecloths, handbags, tea cosies, pillows and dolls all bear traditional Turkish motifs, and are eagerly snapped up by tourists. Locals, finding the idea of a foreigner creating traditional goods intriguing, are avid customers as well. Deli Kızın Yeri is one shop in the bazaar that is always crowded with curious customers.

BROWSE AT THE BOOK MARKET

30 Dilmen Kitabevi

Sahaflar Çarşısı Sokak 20

If your newly acquired (or revived) interest in Ottoman art requires further reading, be sure to pay a visit to the historic Sahaflar Çarşısı. Though the antiquarian book bazaar now caters primarily to the nearby university, Dilmen Kitabevi, the oldest shop within the bazaar, still has something different to offer. According to owner, Ayşegül Manav, the new generation of shopkeepers has shifted its focus on to more profitable subjects. Dilmen, however, continues to stock rare and unusual books, primarily histories of the Ottoman Empire and traditional Turkish handicrafts. Interesting travel books are also to be found.

31 Süleymaniye Camii

Prof. Sıddık Sami Onar Caddesi

Le Corbusier described Mimar Sinan as one of only two architects 'who actually understood the concept of space.' Surrounded by the magical atmosphere of Süleymaniye Camii, it is difficult to disagree. Built in honour of Süleyman the Magnificent and completed in 1557, the mosque stands on Istanbul's highest hill and dominates the skyline. Its four minarets indicate that Süleyman was the fourth Ottoman sovereign since the conquest. Enter through the northwest door (rather than the usual southwest door) into the courtyard, and after visiting the tombs of Süleyman and Roxelana just behind the mosque, have a peek at the breathtaking views of the Golden Horn. Inside, Sinan's architectural genius is evidenced by the immense space, exquisite stained-glass windows (supplied by İbrahim the Mad), and perfect acoustics.

32 Ayrancı Sokağı

Ayrancı Sokağı

A well-kept Ottoman neighbourhood, Ayrancı Sokağı is lined with adjacent old wooden houses that invite visitors to step back into history. One of the first Muslim settlements in Istanbul, it has somehow managed to preserve its character against the ravages of time and over-eager city planners. Freshly-laundered clothes flutter from balconies, old women watch the few tourists wander past, and children play happily in the street. It is hard to believe you are in 21st-century Istanbul.

33 Zeyrek Camii + Zeyrekhane

İbadethane Arkası Sokak 10

One of most important Byzantine landmarks in Istanbul is the 12th-century Church of the Pantocrator, now known as Zeyrek Camii. Originally built for the wife of John II Comnenus, the church became a Roman imperial residence, and ultimately a mosque. Today Zeyrek Camii, the city's second-largest mosque, is in total ruins. But some internal decoration is preserved, including the magnificent marble mosaic pavement. Also occupying the hilltop location, just in front of the mosque, is Zeyrekhane, housed in a recently (over-)restored mansion, which offers traditional Ottoman fare with *sufi* music softly playing in the background against fabulous views of the Golden Horn.

34 Fatih Karadeniz Pidecisi

Büyük Karaman Caddesi 57

Pide is a pizza-like dish prepared primarily with minced meat or cheese, and is best done in Turkey's Black Sea region. Since 1957, a native of the area, Mehmet Yazıcı, has been offering Istanbulians the crispy *pides* of his homeland. Necessary ingredients, such as cheese and butter, are imported from the region as well. The basic décor might leave something to be desired, but the deliciousness of the *pides* more than makes up for it.

35 Cibalikapı Balıkçısı

Abdülezel Paşa Caddesi 7

Located on the western shore of the Golden Horn is an old wooden house with life buoys hanging on its façade. This is Cibalikapı Balıkçısı, a seafood *meyhane* with stunning panorama views encompassing Galata Kulesi (p. 24) and Topkapı Sarayı. The interior is purposefully basic, with wooden tables and painted yellow brick walls. Constantly playing in the background are ancient LPs of equally ancient Turkish and Greek *rebetikos*, adding to the neighbourly atmosphere. The food is based, as is that of any decent *meyhane*, on Greek *meze* and hot appetizers, of which grilled octopus and unsliced calamari are the specialities. The fish is fresh and tasty, and cooked over an oak wood fire, which makes it even tastier.

36 Bulgar Kilisesi (Sveti Stefan)

Mürsel Paşa Caddesi 87

Just a few blocks away from the Greek Orthodox Patriarchate stands one of Istanbul's most remarkable churches. This neo-Gothic church dedicated to St Stephen of the Bulgars dates from 1871, and was made entirely from iron, cast in Vienna and shipped across the Black Sea. The local story is that the Bulgarian Orthodox community, seized by nationalistic fervour, wanted to leave the Greek Orthodox Patriarchate and build its own church. Sultan Abdülaziz, not overly enamoured with the idea, agreed on the seemingly impossible condition that construction be finished in one month. Had Abdülaziz heard of the term 'prefabricated', the outcome might have been very different.

37 Darüzziyafe

145

HANGOVER CURE
38 Tarihi Haliç İşkembecisi
Abdülezel Paşa Caddesi 315

Tripe soup with garlic vinegar is the ultimate Turkish hangover cure, probably why so many of the restaurants listing this item on their menus are 24-hour establishments. Housed in a 600-year-old building just a few steps from the Greek Orthodox Patriarchate, Tarihi Haliç İşkembecisi is one such place. Owner Recep Sarı, who also co-owns the Kör Agop fish restaurant in touristy Kumkapı, has decorated the interior with items collected from his Anatolian adventures, including several guns hanging on the walls. Apart from the tripe soup, also on offer is the Ottoman dessert *zerde* (rosewater, saffron, starch and rice).

ONE PORTION IS NEVER ENOUGH
39 Köfteci Arnavut
Mürsel Paşa Caddesi 155

There are only six formica tables (painted red, yellow and blue) at Köfteci Arnavut, and the menu offers nothing more than lentil and tripe soup, meatballs, and, on certain days, fried liver. Even so, the restaurant, whose name translates as 'Albanian meatballs,' has a turnover that would be the envy of McDonald's. The seventy-year-old establishment, once called Mavi Köşe (Blue Corner), acquired its present name through word-of-mouth (there is no signboard outside), as its Albanian owners make meatballs and little else. The atmosphere is that of a typical artisan eatery, but the well-heeled of Istanbul also flock to its tables. In the old days, the café was popular for its early morning 'call-to-prayer' soups. Unfortunately, today Köfteci Arnavut is only open from 11 a.m to 3 p.m.

PRINCESS OF LEGEND
40 Panaghia Mouchliotissa (Moğolların Meryemi)
Sadrazam Ali Paşa Caddesi

Located in the steep street that winds up to the Greek Orthodox Patriarchate, Panaghia Mouchliotissa is the only Byzantine church still functioning as a Greek Orthodox place of worship. The church takes its name from the legend of Princess Maria, who was sent in the 13th century as a bride for the Mongolian emperor. Following her intended's unexpected death, Maria returned home and

became a nun. Although legend would have it that Maria was the founder of the church, the structure dates back to an earlier period. Nonetheless, the church is still known in Turkish as 'St Mary of the Mongols'.

IMPERIAL AUTHENTICITY
41 Asitane Restaurant

140

CRYSTAL BALL
42 Mihrimah Sultan Camii
Hoca Çakır Caddesi

Named after the favourite daughter of Süleyman the Magnificent, Mihrimah Sultan Camii is yet another work by Sinan, built *c*. 1562–65. It is strategically located within the Walled City at Edirnekapı on the highest of Istanbul's seven hills, thus enabling its minarets to be as close as possible to the sky. Thanks to its remarkable architecture, with 161 windows and only four arches supporting the vast dome, the mosque is vast and spacious on the inside, and glows like a crystal ball on the outside. Badly damaged by earthquakes in the 18th and 19th centuries, the complex was restored, with varying results, each time. Recent attempts have been made to reconstruct the mosque's attendant buildings.

DUNGEONS BUT NO DRAGONS
43 Anemas Zindanları
Dervişzade Caddesi

The Anemas dungeons, located behind the İvaz Efendi mosque and part of the ruined Blachernae Palace, have long been a favourite film location of the Turkish movie industry, doubtless inspired by their grisly past. Two late Byzantine emperors met their untimely ends here, and several more were unwilling guests. Formed by fourteen cells with two basement floors underneath, the prison is named after an Arabic-Byzantine soldier imprisoned here after unwisely rebelling against the emperor Alexios. With its unusual architecture, and despite its somewhat murky atmosphere, the dungeons are well worth a visit – so long as you remember your flashlight.

COFFEE BREAK
44 Pierre Loti Café

154

45 Rahmi M Koç Müzesi
Hasköy Caddesi 27

Now housed in an 18th-century naval foundry, Rahmi M Koç Müzesi is Turkey's first major museum dedicated to the history of transport, industry and communications. Showcasing the private collection of Turkey's leading industrialist, the museum proved so popular that it soon spilled over into the neighbouring historic Hasköy Dockyard. The collection ranges from the small (gramophone needles) to the gargantuan (the remains of a US bomber, shot down in the Second World War). On display are such landmarks of modern transportation as the Penny Farthing bicycle (1870) and the Ford Model T (1918), and even a submarine, moored in the Golden Horn. An interactive gallery allows children to sit behind the wheel of a vintage car, or try their hand at science experiments under the watchful eye of the resident teacher. Two excellent restaurants, Café du Levant and Halat, provide outdoor seating overlooking the water. The museum closes at 5 p.m. Tuesday to Friday and 7 p.m. on weekends, but the restaurants are open until midnight. All three are closed Mondays.

Çukurcuma
Cihangir

Cihangir and Çukurcuma form the trendy heart of Beyoğlu, bursting with nightclubs, cafés, shops, meyhanes and bars, all vying to lure Istanbul's youth and tourists into parting with their cash. Cihangir, the bohemian neighbourhood of the city, is the namesake of the young son of Süleyman the Magnificent. When the boy died as a child, Süleyman ordered a mosque to be built in his honour on a hill overlooking the Bosphorus, the Golden Horn and the Sea of Marmara. In 1720, construction of the mosque finished and the story of the district of Cihangir began.

During the early years of its history, Cihangir was home to a thriving population of Greek, Jewish and Armenian communities, but in the 1970s it experienced a downturn in its fortunes, and became an increasingly rough and marginalized area. The 1990s ushered in a period of revival for the district (as the decade did for much of the city), and professionals, artists and journalists began flocking to the neighbourhood and its picturesque apartments. Today, Cihangir maintains a friendly, small-town vibe, and its family-run stores and laid-back cafés, offering everything from early morning coffee to late night snacks, have ensured that the area has become popular with the city's café society. Located on Akarsu Yokuşu, Cafe Symrna (p. 57) is a true Cihangir classic, and newcomer Leyla (p. 57) attracts an ever-increasing crowd of devotees. Doğa Balık (p. 57), also on Akarsu Yokuşu, is one of Istanbul's finest fish restaurants.

Often referred as the 'SoHo of Istanbul,' Çukurcuma, a neighbourhood next to Cihangir and whose border is located precisely at the wall of the Galatasaray High School in Beyoğlu, is without doubt the most colourful part of the city. With a history dating back to the 16th century, the district takes its name from the Çukurcuma mosque, built in 1541 by ubiquitous royal architect, Mimar Sinan. Settled by Jews, Armenians, Italians, French and Muslims, the area thrives as a diverse and cosmopolitan community, and the melting-pot of cultures adds to the already vibrant atmosphere. Until recently Çukurcuma was showing signs of neglect and was sorely in need of a makeover. Following the initiatives of a few enterprising artists and designers in recent years, elegant art galleries and design emporiums now rub shoulders with the old junk shops in its narrow, twisting alleys.

Today Çukurcuma, together with Cihangir, attracts a new generation of bohemians. Faikpaşa Yokuşu, one of Çukurcuma's most popular streets, is a good place to start a visit to the neighbourhood, whether you are in search of an antique bargain or a decent meal. Strolling through the district is always an adventure, and you never know what awaits you at your next step.

RETRO HOME

1 18

Akyol Sokak 13/A

Opened by architect Selçuk Arıkan in 2001, this small shop offers stylish furniture and home accessories from the 1950s, '60s and '70s, encompassing everything from Murano glassware to leather sofas. Differing from other vintage stores in the city in its excellent stock, only the most elegant objects find a place in the U-shaped premises. Most of the items are original, but there are some reproductions with more wallet-friendly price tags. Paintings from the same period are also on offer, and large canvases by the owner himself complete the décor. The shop's cat, who accompanies visitors on their wanders through the store, was chosen as Cihangir's most beautiful moggy by a local newspaper. Unfortunately, she is not for sale.

LITTLE GERMANY

2 Kay's

Güneşli Sokak 32

Although in business since 1998, Kay's is a well-kept secret, even from the inhabitants of this city. The small café-bar, located on a quiet corner in the friendly neighbourhood of Cihangir, is decorated in the style of a German pub and is beloved by Istanbul's nearly 4,000 German residents. With green and red leather banquettes, wooden tables, and rather odd metal accessories adorning the walls, Kay's offers a cosy environment in which to enjoy the delicious (and enormous) meat dishes, washed down with large steins of German beer. Kay's also serves German speciality dishes on fixed days, including *sauerbraten mit spaetzle* (Thursdays). If you are after *kasseler mit sauerkraut*, be sure to visit on Fridays.

BOHEMIAN OASIS

3 5. Kat

Soğancı Sokak 7

The best time of year to enjoy this eclectic restaurant, whether for a drink or a meal, is on a calm summer evening, as the views from the terrace, sweeping from the Bosphorus bridge to historic Sultanahmet, are truly breathtaking. Located in the artistic district of Cihangir, 5. Kat (5th Floor), the magical bohemian atmosphere (think beaded curtains, burning candles, vivid colours and pictures of kittens) offers international cuisine on a large scale. As well as Turkish items, the menu offers dishes from Indian, Thai, Cambodian and Italian cuisines,

among others. The owner (and former actress) Yasemin Alkaya cooks the majority of the meals herself, with a little help from her mother.

A LITTLE PIZZA ITALY
4 Miss Pizza
Havyar Sokak 7

Miss Pizza is reminiscent of one of the old, family-run pizzerias that crowd the narrow streets of countless Italian cities. Despite being neither old nor run by an Italian family, nor even in Italy, this Istanbulian version is certainly worthy of the tradition. Owner Selen Akınal is a well-known name on the city's entertainment scene, and she and her husband are famous for hosting Saturday night parties at the Sürmeli Hotel's rooftop disco. At Miss Pizza, the *pizza roka* (ricotta, mozzarella, parmigiano, rocket and marinated tomato) and the *pizza funghi* (porcini mushrooms marinated in truffle oil, gorgonzola and mozzarella) are especially delicious, but with every ingredient imported from Italy and eaten in a setting as intimate as this, everything on the menu is hard to resist.

VINTAGE TREASURE
5 Altı
Anahtar Sokak 15

Altı began life as a vintage clothing shop with a small café, but the café has increased in popularity and slowly but surely has begun to take over the premises. Istanbul had very few second-hand clothing stores when Altı opened its doors in 2001, and it quickly became a treasure chest for adventurous fashionistas who coveted its dresses, coats and accessories, which date back to the 1930s. The peacefully quiet café, famous for its cakes and herbal teas, is located at the rear of the store. *Ayranaşı*, a cold soup made with yoghurt, is the highlight of the summer menu. At weekends, Altı's café is a good place to enjoy leisurely breakfasts over newspapers and a game of Scrabble.

CHEESECAKE AND CHANDELIERS

6 Symrna + Symrna Patisserie

Akarsu Yokuşu 29 and Yeni Yuva Sokak 2/1

Sibel Eren, the owner of Cihangir's most popular café-restaurant and the newly-opened patisserie, is also the designer of the venues' interiors. The original Symrna opened in 2002, and has become a magnet for the local bohemian population, who regularly come for the steak with Roquefort sauce and stuffed chicken breast with mozzarella, along with ice-cold lemonade on summer days. The brick-walled bar in the centre of the room, the myriad mirrors in varying shapes and sizes adorning the walls, and the bookcases filled with collectibles create a homey atmosphere. The more flamboyant interior of the patisserie is a riot of red, mint green and pale blue, together with tartan-covered sofas and chandeliers (the best one of these is in the loo). It is a wonderful place to stop for coffee and a bite of one of Symrna's delicious cheesecakes.

ARTISTIC CAFÉ-BAR

7 Leyla

Akarsu Yokuşu 46

A new addition to the boho-chic scene of Cihangir is café-bar Leyla, which has quickly become a popular meeting spot for Istanbul's intellectuals. Owned by famous Turkish actress Deniz Türkali, Leyla (both a common Turkish name and a state of expectant intoxication) can be found on the ground floor of the Hotel Zurich, which also houses the Doğa Balık restaurant (below). The bar is located in the middle of the room, enabling thirsty drinkers to reach it easily from each corner of the café. In the mornings, Leyla serves a set-menu breakfast (with each breakfast named after a city), posted on the enormous blackboard covering one wall.

GOING HERBAL

8 Doğa Balık

Akarsu Yokuşu 46

Though Cihangir is not at the top of everyone's list of favourite neighbourhoods for seafood dining, Doğa Balık is doing its best to change this. Opening in 1995 and located in the Hotel Zurich, this discreet restaurant serves an enormous selection of herbs (mostly from the Aegean and Black Sea regions), and hot appetizers including fish and calamari cakes. When it comes to cooking the seasonal fish (served with garlic and olive oil), owner İbrahim Soğukdağ takes a hands-on role in the kitchen, which, he claims, is what it makes his restaurant so special.

The food is good, the view from the seventh floor is perfect and the service never fails. What more could any gourmand ask for?

SAY CHEESE!

9 Antre Gourmet Shop

Akarsu Yokuşu 52

Antre Gourmet Shop, founded in 2000 by two friends with a shared passion for cheese, is beloved not only of Cihangir residents, but also of gourmets throughout the city. This tiny shop carries around forty different kinds of local Turkish cheese, and offers a wide selection of olive oil, jam, natural yoghurt, honeycomb and imported charcuterie goods, as well as coffee and Turkish *meze*. The friendly staff will gladly help visitors in navigating the well-organized wooden shelves.

CAVERN OF WINE

10 La Cave

Sıraselviler Caddesi 207

It would be pointless to deny the fact that the best wines come from France, Italy and California. However, as the fifth largest wine-producer in the world, Turkey's recent contributions to the international wine répertoire has made sommeliers and connoisseurs sit up and take notice. La Cave on the busy Sıraselviler Caddesi is one of the first speciality wine stores in Turkey, and for those interested in Turkish wines, it is an address to note. Covering 100 square metres, the store offers a vast selection of Anatolian wine, grouped according to their types on large wooden shelves, as well as olive oils, foreign cheeses and cigars. Visitors can taste away to their hearts' content while chatting with owner Esat Ayhan, a man who seems to know more about wine than anyone else in Istanbul.

11 Savoy Pastanesi
Sıraselviler Caddesi 181-183A

Savoy Pastanesi is a Cihangir institution. For many of the neighbourhood's residents, each day starts with breakfast at this established patisserie. Since opening in 1950, long before the arrival of the Starbucks empire, Savoy has been offering freshly-baked cakes to visitors who linger in the first floor café, or commuters who drop in for a pastry on their way to work. Although a less than sympathetic refurbishment in 2003 has robbed Savoy of some of its nostalgic atmosphere, the same savoury smell still lures in passers-by in their hundreds to sample its delights.

12 Asri Turşucusu
Ağa Hamamı Caddesi 29/A

Located at the point where Cihangir ends and Çukurcuma begins is Asri Turşucusu, the oldest pickle producer in the city. Owner Vahdettin Çelikli, who founded the company in 1938, is now 90 years old. Deciding to take it a bit easier in the future, he recently passed on his secret formula to the younger generation of the family. There are around twenty-five different kinds of pickles displayed in glass jars around the shop, ranging from common varieties (cucumber and cabbage) to the more obscure (okra and beetroot). The shop is closed during the summer months when the family is busy pickling for next season. Even if you not buy a jar to take back home, order a glass of *şalgam suyu* (pickle juice) or *boza* (a fermented millet drink) to sip on your way to Çukurcuma's bric-a-brac shops.

13 Evihan
Altıpatlar Sokak 8

This cosy shop offers hand-made accessories, beaded glass ornaments, and delicate authentic garments. Following a career in tourism and wanting to unleash her inner artist, owner Kristin Evihan attended Michaela Koppl's glass-bead workshop in Beykoz in 2003. Three months later, she opened Evihan to display her own creations, and soon added pieces by other designers. Among the shop's treasures are accessories designed especially for Evihan, which combine fragments of İznik tile and silver. The handbags and shoes are also exceptional. Like the store, each object is the only one of its kind.

14 Zaman Tüneli
Turnacıbaşı Sokak 80

A tiny store with a huge stock, Zaman Tüneli is one of the most popular spots in Çukurcuma. Originally occupying a mere 16 square metres, the store has recently gained an upstairs extension. Owner İlker Eryıldız has been collecting tin toys and other memorabilia since childhood, and today happily holds court among his collectibles. The toys date back to the 1940s, and most of the other items, including telephones, radios, lighting fixtures and a few pieces of furniture, are from 1970s. Also on display is a wide variety of popular and hard-to-find Coca-Cola collectibles. Collectors are sure to find their hearts' desire at Zaman Tüneli, but navigating the over-crowded store is another matter altogether.

15 Halide d.
Turnacıbaşı Sokak 71/1

Halide Didem has been designing interiors, including the Mövenpick Hotel in Levent, for the last fifteen years. In 2002 she opened Halide d. to showcase her own unique designs, ranging from coffee cups to light fixtures, along with those of local artists. A year later Didem took the bold step of moving from Nişantaşı to Çukurcuma, believing that Çukurcuma's bohemian atmosphere was a more suitable setting for her vision. Also on display at Halide d. are sculptures by Tuğrul Selçuk, Yücel Kale and Suzi Hug Levi and paintings by İsmail Acar and Kezban Arca Batıbeki. Along with the contents of her shop, Halide Didem also designed the interior of the store's two-storey showroom.

16 Suzanne Simon
Faikpaşa Yokuşu 1

Çukurcuma is rapidly becoming Istanbul's answer to New York's bohemian SoHo, particularly the historic Faikpaşa Yokuşu. Like Marita Bitlis, the Irish owner of Caffe della Suda, an English-style café famous for its breakfasts, American textile designer Suzanne Simon has also chosen to settle in the street and set up an atelier to manufacture her fabric designs, inspired by the embroidered decoration of Ottoman textiles. Prior to going solo, Simon worked for the Division line of fashion house Vakko's younger label, Vakkorama. Today, Simon's products are sold to luxury stores abroad, including Barneys New York.

HATS & HANDBAGS
17 Mine Kerse
Faikpaşa Yokuşu 1/A

A former assistant to fashion designer Ümit Ünal (p. 168), Mine Kerse set up her own atelier and shop in 2004. Inside the relaxed atmosphere of her showroom, she presents a limited collection of beautifully crafted hats and handbags made from felt and leather, and unusual materials such as machine straps. Mine Kerse works at the studio above the shop, reached by a steel ladder from the ground-floor showroom. A shoe collection of one-off designs is also on the way.

ART FOR SALE
18 Art Shop
Faikpaşa Yokuşu 7/2

In this two-storey gallery run by Jale Odabaşı, works by young local artists and designers remain on display until they are sold. The pieces on offer are a mixed collection of contemporary applied arts, including ceramics, furniture, jewelry, pâpier-maché, sculpture and metalwork. With its white walls and wooden floors on the ground level, and brick walls in the basement, the gallery presents a calm and peaceful atmosphere. During warm days, the space opens onto a beautiful garden, overlooking the historic Ağa Hamamı.

TREASURE PLEASURE
19 A La Turca
166

NATURAL DESIGN
20 Accenturc
174

TREASURES FROM YESTERYEAR
21 Pied de Poule
Faikpaşa Yokuşu 19/1

A visit to this corner shop in the heart of Çukurcuma is like having a good old rummage in your grandmother's wardrobe. On display are clothes dating from the 1930s, hats, gloves and leather handbags with wooden straps, as well as vintage decorative items, ranging from porcelain to French armchairs. Every item in the shop can be purchased or hired out. Owner Şelale Gültekin started collecting historic clothes from family members as a hobby, and as the collection outgrew her own wardrobe, the hobby turned into a profitable business. Gültekin also makes delicately embroidered cushions, which are among the stores most covetable items. The black and white photographs of Gültekin adorning the walls were taken by Nuri Bilge Ceylan, the well-known Turkish director.

WE MAKE COFFEE
22 Koyu Kahve
Hayriye Sokak 5/2–3

Koyu Kahve is a café-restaurant that is never scarce on customers, and each shopping trip to the alternative stores of Hayriye Sokak is finished off with a cuppa here. Located at the top of the stairs leading to the Galatasaray *hamamı*, its wooden tables, long and spacious ba, and painted brick walls are domed with a high, bare-brick ceiling. The restaurant section, with its light wooden furniture set against old black and white tiles, offers a menu of salads, pasta, grilled meat and chicken. During the summer months, tables are set up on the streetside pavement.

POCKET-SIZED DESIGN STORE
23 Eşik Design
Hayriye Sokak 20/2

Located in the trendy area where Çukurcuma meets
Galatasaray, Eşik Design was founded by three interior
architects and two fashion designers. The showroom is
rather small, but its three-storey space allows shoppers to
roam freely. On sale are accessories such as frames,
ashtrays and clocks, as well as light fixtures and a few
pieces of furniture. Items of note include 'Hexagon', a
coffee-table with a plexiglass top decorated with Ottoman
motifs, and 'Dumble', a floor-lighting unit. There is also a
small selection of fashion items, including T-shirts,
tracksuits and hats, from alternative European labels.

URBAN GEAR
24 Bis Wear
Hayriye Sokak 20/3

The owners of Bis Wear, two sisters, started designing hats
while they were still students. Following the success of
these hats, they abandoned prospective engineering
careers and opened their first store within one of Beyoğlu's
historic arcades, selling export surplus along with their own
designs. With its unusual fabrics and simple but stylish
forms, Bis Wear quickly gained a dedicated clientele, who
also snapped up the matching shoes, handbags and belts.
In 2003, Bis Wear moved to its present location. The small
shop within the arcade is still open, but for the real thing,
take the ride to Hayriye Sokak.

KNOCK ON WOOD
25 Stoa
172

A FRENCH AFFAIR
26 Fransız Sokağı
• Dilara'sabra Cadabra, no. 6

In 2003 the historic mansions of the old Cezayir Sokağı
were renovated one-by-one and painted in ice-cream
colours. Renamed Fransız Sokağı (French Street) to reflect
the new French-style cafés and boutiques, the street is
more Disneyland than Dordogne, and still receives endless
criticism. If you are suddenly feeling peckish, bypass the
cafés and head to Dilara'sabra Cadabra. Dilara Erbay, the
owner and chef of this three-storey eatery, refuses to be a
part of the concept street, and, together with her two co-
chefs, has devised an experimental menu using only the
freshest organic ingredients.

Harbiye
Nişantaşı
Teşvikiye
Maçka

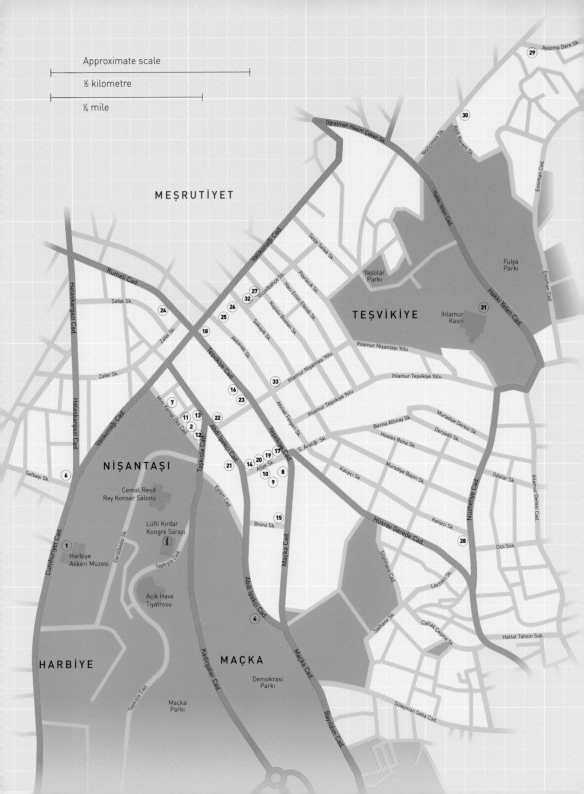

For Istanbul's savvy fashionistas, the triangle of Nişantaşı, Teşvikiye and Maçka north of Taksim Meydanı is the heart of Istanbul, offering everything needed for a shop-til-you-drop experience. Shopaholics can flex their plastic at the endless variety of designer boutiques and luxury goods stores, and later collapse with the fruits of their commercial labour for a restorative coffee at the popular cafés and restaurants that line the district's trendy streets. For those requiring a more cultural experience, the neighbourhood also boasts some of the city's best art galleries.

Taking its name from the five marksman's obelisks (nişantaşı) in the courtyard of the Teşvikiye mosque, Nişantaşı has always been popular, first with sultans of the Ottoman empire, and, following the declaration of a republic, with society's new élite. Designated as a residential area by Abdülmecid I in the 1920s, enormous villas immediately began springing up on farmland once used as the royal hunting grounds. As the neighbourhood sky-rocketed in popularity, the houses were replaced with apartment buildings, which soon spread out to the neighbouring Teşvikiye and Maçka. Today the area's appeal is greater than ever. This is especially true of the Abdi İpekçi Caddesi, and a stroll past its elegant shop windows feels like a front-row seat at the most glamorous Parisian fashion show. Nişantaşı's modern appearance is due (natch) to redevelopment in the 1990s, which attracted such luxury brands as Louis Vuitton, Tiffany and Escada to its spruced-up streets. The rents are high and the price tags (and traffic) are alarming, but Nişantaşı remains a firm favourite with the city's urban middle-class.

Once visitors have wearied of shopping and have deposited their bags at one of the nearby five-star hotels, Maçka Parkı and Demokrasi Parkı, together forming the district's back garden, offer acres of green open spaces for relaxation and people-watching. At the main entrance of the park stands the Maçka Çeşmesi (Maçka Fountain), built in 1901 by Italian architect Raimondo D'Aranco. Just outside the park in Maçka Caddesi is the early 20th-century Maçka Palas, designed by another Italian, Giulio Mongeri, and which houses both Gucci and Giorgio Armani, along with the sleekly elegant Armani Caffe (p. 158). The area has also recently acquired something of a reputation as Istanbul's 'Congress Valley'. Located behind the Harbiye Askeri Müzesi (p. 68) are the Lüftı Kırdar Kongre Sarayı, an international congress centre which also houses popular restaurant Loft (p. 68), the Cemal Reşit Rey Konser Salonu (concert hall) and the Atatürk Kültür Merkezi (culture centre), all benefiting from the neighbourhood's recent facelift and steady stream of well-to-do visitors.

ARMS AND THE BAND

1   Harbiye Askeri Müzesi
Valikonağı Caddesi

A former military school that counts Atatürk among its
more illustrious alumni, Harbiye Askeri Müzesi has
functioned since 1993 as a military museum and cultural
centre. Equipped with conference rooms and exhibition
galleries, the museum has a large collection of Ottoman
rifles, some of which date back to the 15th century,
embroidered campaign pavilions, armour for both cavalry
and horses, and even furniture constructed out of bayonets.
The museum's main attraction is the world's first-ever
military band, which plays old Turkish instruments whilst
dressed in full Ottoman costume. Performances are held
Wednesday-Sunday at 3 p.m.

FIT FOR A SULTAN

2   Hünkar
Mim Kemal Öke Caddesi 21

First opened in 1950, Hünkar has been serving classic
Ottoman cuisine ever since. Its fame and popularity
ensured that it quickly outgrew its original location in
the conservative district of Fatih, and the restaurant moved
twice before landing in its present spot in Nişantaşı. In a
nod to the restaurant's past, owner and chef Feridun
Ürgümü has incorporated street signs from the earlier
locations into the modern décor. For those who don't read
Turkish, dishes on the menu are visible at the counter in
front of the kitchen. Favourites include *Hünkar Beğendi*
(stuffed aubergine) and lamb with quince, and for diners
with a sweet tooth, the deliciously toothsome *irmik helvası*
(semolina saffron with pistachio helva).

LOFTY ASPIRATIONS

3   Loft
Lütfi Kırdar Kongre Sarayı

A chic restaurant housed within a convention centre does
not seem like a marriage made in heaven, but since the day
it opened its doors in 2002, Loft has claimed the most
sought-after tables in the city. A branch of the Borsa
restaurant group (p. 149), Loft serves up international
and traditional Turkish dishes with a modern twist. Owner
Ümit Özkanca is a graduate of the French Culinary
Institute in New York, and the décor of his restaurant,
designed by Nazlı Gönensay, has a Manhattan flavour,
with its large bar at the centre and leather banquettes for
those who prefer to distance themselves from the
maddeningly noisy crowd.

CONTEMPORARY DESIGN EMPORIUM

4 Derin Design

Abdi İpekçi Caddesi 77/1

Aziz Sarıyer founded his cutting-edge contemporary furniture emporium Derin in the early 1980s, and the initial showroom offered an international range of items from such manufacturers as Memphis, Cappelini and Moroso. Soon after his son (also named Derin) joined the firm in 1998, Sarıyer moved the showroom to a loft-like space in the same street, and the company developed its own line of furniture. Derin Design's collection of sofas, chairs, tables, beds and storage units has a refined, slick and futuristic look, strongly influenced by contemporary Italian style, and is featured in many international design periodicals.

DINE IN STYLE

5 Boğaziçi Borsa Restaurant

149

COMFORT IN SIMPLICITY

6 Bentley Hotel

126

NO MADDER WHAT

7 Güneş Halı

Mim Kemal Öke Caddesi 5

The owner of the eponymous Güneş Halı, one of the oldest and most elegant carpet shops in Nişantaşı, has been the leading female rug dealer in Istanbul for twenty-five years. Each hand-woven Turkish carpet comes with its own story, as the young women of Anatolia have patiently knotted rugs for their trousseau chests for centuries. The beauty and symmetry of the geometrical patterns, and the rich pigments of madder dye, make each carpet a work of art. Both antique and modern rugs are available, as are cushions. Only the brave venture into Güneş Halı, as a visit to the shop might result in a change of décor at home.

CORPORATE COLLECTION

8 Milli Reasürans Sanat Galerisi

Teşvikiye Caddesi 43–57

This corporate art gallery curated by Amelie Edgü is part of the huge business complex belonging to the Milli Reasürans company, and has been organizing exhibitions and retrospectives since opening in 1994. Its exhibition devoted to the 75th anniversary of the Turkish Republic, accompanied by a catalogue published by the gallery,

was a particular success. Situated at the junction of Nişantaşı's two main streets, the Milli Reasürans Sanat Galerisi, which incorporates a library and an auditorium, is never short of visitors.

NEIGHBOURHOOD BAR
9 Touchdown
Milli Reasürans Çarşısı 61/11

In 1993 two friends, who met while studying architecture at university, launched Touchdown in the Milli Reasürans Pasajı, an arcade filled with cafés, bookstores, clothing and shoe shops and a cinema. Originally founded to entertain the owners' friends, the small café-bar quickly became hugely popular. After more than a decade, Touchdown still maintains both its original staff and décor (an homage to American football). Regulars' birthdays are mentioned in the monthly events list posted on the door and on the website. During the summer months, Touchdown opens onto the stairs of the arcade to make room for everybody.

DESIGNER DREAMS
10 Ayça
Atiye Sokak 7/8

This showroom-cum-atelier is located on the second floor of an apartment building, but adventurous fashionistas have no difficulties beating a path to its doors to snap up Ayça's fun and colourful, if disturbingly surreal, designs. Ayça herself is a young and highly creative fashion designer with a CV that bears the names of St Martin's in London and the Marangoni Institute. She also designs jewelry and paints her 'dreams' – literally – onto enormous canvases. The setting of her showroom reflects Ayça's imaginary world, and instead of curtains, the windows are covered with Barbie dolls painted in white from head to toe.

SOUFFLÉ GOOD
11 Mimkemal 19
148

MODERN LUXURY
12 Park Şamdan
144

13 Urart
Abdi İpekçi Caddesi 18/1

Due to the outrageous rents, turnover on Istanbul's most prestigious street is startlingly high. But Urart has survived the mean streets of Nişantaşı for over thirty years. This gallery-cum-store reproduces and reinterprets ancient Anatolian and Central Asian artefacts, creating jewelry designs that whisk the buyer back into history. In partnership with the Istanbul Arkeoloji Müzesi (p. 36), Urart holds exhibitions at historic locations such as Beylerbeyi Sarayı (p. 115) and Anadolu Medeniyetleri Müzesi (Museum of Anatolian Civilizations). A collection of reproductions by Urart, based on an exhibition of ancient Mediterranean and Indian artefacts at New York's Metropolitan Museum, is sold in the museum's stores worldwide.

JEWEL GALLERY
14 Ela Cindoruk – Nazan Pak
Atiye Sokak 14

Unusual and modern ornaments are to be found in this small gallery and shop, co-owned by two designers. Before joining forces in 1993, Ela Cindoruk studied jewelry design at New York's Parsons School of Design, and Nazan Pak trained in metalwork at the atelier of Levon-Raffi Sadyan, in the Grand Bazaar. Many of the pieces on display are designed by the duo themselves, and the gallery also exhibits and sells works by both local and international artists, including Karin Wagner (felt), Ana Hagopian (paper and cloth), Kaz Robertson (polyester resin), and Mike Abbott & Kim Elwood (metal).

COSMOPOLITAN COCKTAILS
15 Armani Caffe

158

Designer Mehtap Elaidi set up her atelier-cum-shop in 2000 to target the modern young woman. Using different fabrics sourced from the domestic market and around the world, Elaidi creates unique collections that are sought after by the city's followers of fashion. Her simple cuts and quirky details have loyal fans, mostly locals seeking to add a little individuality to their wardrobes. With the recent addition of a new bag collection, Elaidi continues to widen her product range while maintaining her individual style.

Just a stone's throw from a Nişantaşı landmark (the Marksman's Obelisk, which lends its name to the district), a shop window filled with colourful fruit glacé catches the eye. This twenty-five-year-old family-run establishment is an old-fashioned patisserie, beloved of its local clientele, that still caters to traditional tastes. The mouth-watering aroma of the chocolate almond cookies nestled on trays on the takeaway counter lures in unsuspecting passers-by. This is not a place to count calories.

ottomanempire

t-shirt

t:(0212) 296 56 19

Regarded as one of the best chefs in the city, former stylist Şemsa Denizsel's talent in the kitchen is evidenced by the number of customers flocking to her tables at Kantin. On the menu are such house specialities as *çıttr* (a thin pizza-like dish) and schnitzel, served in a minimal setting of leather banquettes and wooden tables in the front room, and more tables at the rear with a garden view. The menu is posted on a large blackboard, and Denizsel herself will gladly explain the choices to hungry diners. Recently she joined forces with archaeologist Sinan Aşkın to open Mimkemal 19 (p. 148), also in Nişantaşı.

THE EMPIRE STRIKES BACK
26 Ottoman Empire
Şakayık Sokak 59/1

Among the many chic boutiques to bring a Western-influenced design culture to the neighbourhood, Ottoman Empire dares to be different. The owners (two former brokers and an ad agency creative director) take Ottoman motifs and bring them bang up-to-date with quirky English phrases and pop designs, and the resulting T-shirts immediately gained considerable attention from the area's style-conscious bohos. The tiny shop, located on the ground floor of an apartment building, has a plain, all-white interior that keeps the focus on the limited edition T-shirts.

OTTOMANIA
27 Deniz Tunç Design
Güzelbahçe Sokak 5/1

The beautifully crafted lighting designs and decorative screens make this elegant store a treasure trove for the serious home shopper. Deniz Tunç gave up her career as an art director on film sets to create more permanent items, and, having worked with Zeynep Fadılloğlu (the inspiration behind the interior of London's Chintamani restaurant) in decorating Ulus 29 (p. 143), thought it was time to display her own creations. With strong references to Ottoman motifs, Tunç's line of lighting fixtures is highly original, and a visit to her showroom feels like stepping into a museum of design – apart from the price tags.

NEEDFUL THINGS
28 Gerekli Şeyler
Kalıpçı Sokak 111/1

Most of the items on display at Gerekli Şeyler are imports from Europe and the US, but this store has also created its own Istanbul subculture. Comic books, science fiction, action figures and board games jostle for space on its shelves, and a well-informed and spirited staff are on hand to help you find them. When it opened in 1994, the shop took full advantage of its location next door to the perennially popular Touchdown (p. 71). Curious barflies, and those escaping from the bad weather, were the were the first to venture across Gerekli Şeyler's threshold, and the shop rapidly became the talk of the town. Owner Ahmet Kocaoğlu also publishes Turkish comic books through his own company.

FLOWER POWER
29 Ceremony
Ayazmadere Caddesi 30/1

In 1990 İrem Yargıcı, a member of the Yargıcı family behind the eponymous Turkish fashion chain, set up flower shop Ceremony, drawing on her background in textiles to create unusual combinations of flowers and colours. With attention to such details as containers and ribbons, Ceremony provides aesthetically pleasing floral arrangements to enhance your living space or spice up special occasions.

30 Derishow

173

LITTLE GEM

31 Ihlamur Kasrı

Ihlamur Nişantaşı Yolu

The surrounding linden (*ıhlamur*) trees give their name to this 150-year-old neo-baroque palace. Built for Sultan Abdülmecit as a hunting lodge, each room of this tiny palace is illuminated by crystal chandeliers and heated by porcelain fireplaces. Marble-like stucco blocks covering the walls create perfect acoustics. In the summer, a decent tea garden serves coffee and linden tea, and is a good place in which to admire the baroque façade and nod off under the many trees, some of which are as old as the palace. Horns from the noisy passing traffic will soon bring you back to the present.

IT'S ALL ABOUT FOOD

32 Cook Book

Güzelbahçe Sokak 5/2

For anyone with culinary ambitions, Cook Book is a must. Ebru Suner Ungan and Burcu Pinto, both graduates of Switzerland's International College of Hospitality Administration, started Cook Book as a lunch-time café and bookshop devoted entirely to cookbooks. The dominant open-plan kitchen at the centre produces cuisine from a different country each month, and set menus are planned accordingly. In response to constant requests for recipes, Ungan and Pinto set up cooking courses for groups. Today, Cook Book is a place to find all your culinary needs, from sushi materials to hard-to-find sauces.

HOME SWEET HOME

33 Ev+

Ihlamur Nişantaşı Yolu 9/3

Yael Meşulam has been selling contemporary tableware, glass, ceramics, textiles and accessories at Ev+ since opening her shop in 1993. With simple forms adorning a broad product range, the Ev+ collection has a fresh look and, more importantly, an affordable price list. Most of the goods on display were designed by the owner herself, and sit alongside a few imported glass objects. The staff is friendly and willing to help if you are undecided when choosing the perfect gift for someone special – or for you.

Levent
Etiler
Ulus

Located further north up the Bosphorus from the metropolitan centres of Beyoğlu and Nişantaşı, the three wealthy neighbourhoods of Levent, Etiler and Ulus are far from touristy. Only for those with a stout heart and a stouter wallet, the area offers unforgettable shopping and dining experiences for the seriously spendy.

Of the three suburbs, Levent is the traditional stomping ground of Istanbul's rich and famous. As a result of its continual development and expansion, it has been divided into sections (rather unimaginitively called Levent 1-2-3 and 4), and is primarily a financial district occupied by countless corporate skyscrapers. Located on the ground floor of the Harmancı Giz Plaza, contemporary art gallery Proje 4L (p. 83) provides one of the few cultural respites in the area. Nearby Etiler sports both houses and shops, and is home to several trendy cafés and nightclubs. Along Nispetiye Caddesi, the area's main thoroughfare, most of the private houses have been turned into banks or restaurants. Within walking distance is Turkey's largest shopping mall, the four-storey Akmerkez, which in 1995 was named the Best Shopping Centre in Europe. A more recent claim to fame is that it houses Paper Moon (p. 147), Istanbul's priciest restaurant. Occupying a triangular junction off Nispetiye Caddesi, Akmerkez has two entrances, one of which opens out to Etiler, and the other to Ulus.

Wending their way back down the hillside to residential Ulus, followers of fashion can scrutinize the latest offerings at Ulus Pazarı. An open-air clothing bazaar regularly raided by savvy locals, Ulus Pazarı offers up catwalk looks at bargain basement prices every Thursday. At the bottom of Ahmet Adnan Saygun Caddesi, Ulus Parkı, located on a hill facing the Bosphorus, houses two of Istanbul's most shamelessly romantic restaurants, Ulus 29 (p. 143) and Sunset Grill & Bar (p. 88), both of which offer breathtaking panoramas of the strait along with dinner. Should shopping and proposals not be on the agenda, have a look at Ulus's truly sumptuous hilltop villas. The neighbourhood is as bustling by night as it is by day. Its amazingly varied entertainment scene includes popular Turkish singers taking the stage at various clubs until the first signs of rosy-fingered dawn. The red carpet is always on standby, as is the horde of paparazzi hovering at the exit for a snap of a famous footballer with his new girlfriend. Not far from the Levent-Etiler-Ulus triangle are the peaceful Bosphorus villages of Bebek, Arnavutoköy and Ortaköy, whose wooden seaside cottages and casual meyhanes couldn't be further from the razzle-dazzle of their more glamorous neighbours.

MEDITERRANEAN RIM
1 AzzuR Restaurant + BarAdox
Büyükdere Caddesi 4

QUALITY AND SIMPLICITY
2 Dört Mevsim
Mayadrom Alışveriş Merkezi 34

The interior of the effortlessly elegant AzzuR Restaurant, located on the ground floor of the Mövenpick Hotel, is a mixture of the modern and the classical, but the cuisine is pure Mediterranean Rim. At the intimate, open-plan kitchen, Turkey's first-ever female chef Lorraine Sinclair is on duty. Beef tartare served with black caviar, baby calamari and *halloumi shish*, seafood risotto and seared fillet of salmon are highlights of the menu. Naturally, several flavours of the world-famous Mövenpick ice cream are available for dessert. BarAdox, overlooking the the hotel's tiny garden and the bustling main street, is located next to the hotel's main entrance, and is perfect for an aprés-work Cosmopolitan or Mojito.

Since 1998, Dört Mevsim, housed in the tiny shopping mall Mayadrom, has sold delicate towels, linens, tablecloths and haircare products of its own manufacture, as well as fabrics from London-based Malabar and bath and beauty treats from French company, Durance. This sophisticated shop also designs furniture and provides an interior design service. Owned by two sisters, Şebnem and Meltem Berker, Dört Mevsim's simple but opulent style has many devotees in Istanbul. Their winning formula is to provide fresh and sensual products with prices that won't break the bank.

3 Proje 4L

Harman Sokak Harmancı Giz Plaza

Since its launch in 2001, gallery Proje 4L has filled a contemporary art gap in the city, hosting such events as the debut showing of fashion designer Hussein Chalayan's video installation, *Place to Passage*. Lack of sponsorship led to a brief closure, but Proje 4L was soon back in action in its original premises with a new attitude. Instead of offering a changing programme of exhibitions, it now functions as the permanent gallery space for its founders' private collections. Temporary exhibitions are shown at the newly-added Artvarium.

PIZZA AND A MOVIE

4 Bistrott

Mayadrom Alışveriş Merkezi 47/A

At dinner time, this post-modern bistro is crowded with moviegoers, as the Mayadrom shopping mall also houses one of the best and most luxurious movie theatres in town. During lunch hours Bistrott caters to officeworkers, who enjoy the delicious pizzas to the cacophony of constantly ringing mobile phones. Along with pizza, Bistrott also serves pasta, risotto and tiramisu, all in a setting which is more New York than Istanbul. Owner Cüneyt Kurt is a well-known name on the Istanbul entertainment scene, having been a local DJ in his younger days. Kurt was also the man behind such top-class restaurants as Şans, Bice and Mirror, before setting up the popular Bistrott.

5 Kiliza

4. Gazeteciler Sitesi A 28/2

For culinary adventurers, Kiliza is a must. Set in a villa, this restaurant offers southeastern fare, and takes its name from the ancient word for Kilis, the hometown of owner Nuran Kazaca. The region made its name from its local kebaps, and the menu at Kiliza is heavily weighted in that direction. There are around twenty different varieties, all of which are hot and spicy in the traditional Kilis manner to prevent spoilage in hot weather. Appetizers include *çiğ köfte* (raw meatball) and *içli köfte* (deep-fried, stuffed meatball), and a house speciality is *yuvalama*, an authentic yoghurt soup. *Künefe*, a sweet pastry with melted cheese, is definitely something to leave room for.

BACK TO NATURE

6 City Farm

Mayadrom Alışveriş Merkezi 29

Aware of global fads, Istanbul's stores and restaurants have not been slow in hopping on the organic bandwagon.

A pioneer in Turkey's health-food business, City Farm, founded in 2000 by Karen and Murat Denizel, must take some credit for the ever-increasing popularity of organic produce. On its visually appealing shelves are local fruit and vegetables, spices, soy milk, sea salt, goat's cheese and olive oil products, all accompanied with a certificate of quality. Whether it is a jar of thyme honey or grape molasses you are after, City Farm is your address. And the paper packaging is recycled, too.

COLLEGE LIFE

7 Harvard Café

Seher Yıldızı Sokak 6

If you must blame someone for the avalanche of cafés threatening to take over the city, you might as well blame this one. Since opening doors in 1995, Harvard Café was the first such establishment in Istanbul (along with Nişantaşı's now-defunct Café Keyif). Set in a two-storey villa, Harvard Café was so named due to owner Oğuz Şenol's fondness for Boston and its nearby university. It has a relaxed and casual atmosphere, and the walls are hung with black and white photographs of college life (including

sculls on the Charles River). The menu is divided into sections for crêpes, pasta, pizza and other main dishes, including aubergine steak roll. There is also a vast rear garden for warmer days.

FANTISTICO ITALIANO

8 Da Mario

Dil Hayat Sokak 7

Da Mario is the linchpin in the İstanbul Doors empire's quest for domination of the city's stylish dining scene. The group also owns Vogue (p. 159), Wanna (a pan-Asian eatery-cum-cocktail bar), Angelique (a trendy bar-club) and A'jia (p. 122). The first-ever Italian restaurant to arrive in Istanbul, Da Mario takes its name from its original chef, Mario Parisi, well known for creating delicious southern Italian dishes. Long after his departure, the food still preserves his presence. The cosy setting of Da Mario feels like a private house rather than a restaurant, and well-spaced tables get plenty of light from the large glass windows. Such is the restaurant's popularity with both locals and visitors, that tables spill out into the beautiful garden during summer months.

9 Şütte

Nispetiye Caddesi 52

Opened in 1918 by Herr Schutte and taking its name from the Turkish version of the owner's surname, this deli chain is where most of the city does its charcuterie shopping. Offering a wide range of imported goods, including several varieties of sauces and cheese, the shop also sells local organic produce. Famous for its made-to-order baguette sandwiches, Şütte also has twenty types of *meze* for takeaway lunches. The original Herr Schutte returned to his homeland after the Second World War, and since 1969 the chain has been run by Jifko Eldek.

SPORTY SPICE

10 All Sports Café

Çamlık Sokak 1/2

Whether you are a sports fan or not, the themed décor at All Sports Café is something else. Designed by Hakan Ezer, this café offers a journey through the history of sport, with ancient tennis rackets and wooden skis adorning the walls. The menu offers generous portions of seven different salads (try the Cajun), and main dishes ranging from crèpes to schnitzel. Because the prices are reasonable, the café does a brisk trade throughout the day, from early morning coffee to late night *raki*.

AFFORDABLE DESIGN

11 Dank!

Mayadrom Uptown Alışveriş Merkezi P2 Garaj Katı

For design devotees who revere vintage items for their character and reduced price tag, Dank! is 650 square metres of heaven on earth. Or perhaps under earth, as the shop is housed below ground level in the car park of a shopping arcade. Having moved to larger and easier-to-find premises in 2003, owners Yağmur Sencer and Cahit Musal found that their list of dedicated customers has grown even longer. The ever-changing stock consists of slightly-damaged 1960s and '70s furniture and accessories, all sourced from importers' and manufacturers' warehouses. Recently Dank! added clothing label Dank Giy! (Wear Dank!), which offers second-hand finds and fashion labels' excess stock from past collections.

THE FAMOUS ITALIAN

12 Paper Moon

147

BEDS AND PIECES

13 GES

Esra Sokak G3 Blok D/2

Founded in 2001, home-textile company GES became a global name so quickly that by the time shoppers discovered the showroom, the owners were already sharing first prize with Kenzo Home at Parisian design fair, Maison & Objet. GES (formed by the initials of the three owners' names) offers an exclusive line of linens, bedspreads, cushions and nightgowns, all designed with simplicity and elegance in mind. Modernizing traditional Turkish craftsmanship with hand-made details, the collection offers fabrics specially woven to highlight the sensation of warmth and softness. GES is open by appointment only.

DIAMONDS ARE FOREVER

14 Gilan

Akmerkez Alışveriş Merkezi 123

Founded in 1981 by the Geylan brothers, Muharrem and Ferhan, jewelry house Gilan's designs draw inspiration from Anatolian motifs and the craft traditions of the Ottoman Empire. After opening a by-appointment showroom in New York's Crown Building in addition to its stores in Istanbul, Bursa and Ankara, the company's modern take on Turkey's rich cultural heritage has been winning new fans from international jet-setters. This location is the only Gilan store in Istanbul, and its sophisticated and minimal showroom is perfectly in keeping with the elegant designs.

LET THEM EAT CAKE

15 Foodie

Güzel Konutlar Sitesi 1-2

Peasants ordered by Marie Antoinette to eat cake will be happy to do so at this shop. Pastry chef Emel Başdoğan bakes her sculptural cakes by commission, but a passing visit to her shop won't leave you empty-handed. Apart from the beautifully arty party cakes waiting to be collected, Foodie's counters are lined with trays full of delicious cookies for takeaway munching. Even perpetual dieters are catered to, as the 'zero to zero' cake is prepared with milk-free chocolate and without flour and sugar. But have no fear, it is every bit as delicious as all of the other goodies at Foodie.

24-HOUR EATERY

16 Şayan 24

Nispetiye Caddesi Petrol Sitesi 2

This café is where Istanbul's night owls like to finish their evenings out before heading home, and the busiest hours at Şayan 24 are just before dawn. After long hours of bar hopping and clubbing, revellers retreat here to refuel with the wide variety of high-calorie dishes and desserts. As ever at the city's 24-hour-cafés, the most popular item on the menu is that all-important hangover cure, tripe soup.

PARK LIFE

17 Ulus Parkı

Ulus Parkı

Taking full advantage of its hilltop location in the back garden of Istanbul's posh district, Ulus park has mesmerizing views of the Bosphorus that include the distant silhouettes of Topkapı Sarayı in the old city and Üsküdar on the Asian shore. The park offers recreational grounds for those who wish to spend a relaxing day (rather than their money), as well as a fabulous choice of restaurants. Ulus 29 (p. 143), the city's finest restaurant, and Sunset Grill & Bar (below), the city's most romantic restaurant, are within the park's premises. The park becomes over-crowded on sunny weekends, but early-morning joggers will find they have only the birds for company.

FANTASY FOOD

18 Ulus 29 + Club 29

143

SAY YES!

19 Sunset Grill & Bar

Yol Sokak 2

Due to its lushly romantic setting, this restaurant has earned something of a reputation as a favourite location for proposals, and the management often receives requests to hide rings in the pudding. Sunset Grill & Bar began life eleven years ago as a Californian-fusion restaurant, but over time has adopted an international approach and widened its menu. A member of the James Beard Foundation (the only restaurant in Turkey to be so honoured), Sunset is also famous for possessing a vast wine cellar. The spice garden outside supplies both the kitchen and the bar. In such perfect surroundings, no one would dream of saying 'no.'

The Bosphorus

KİREÇBURNU

TARABYA

YENİKÖY

İSTİNYE

EMİRGAN

RUMELİHİSARI

Emirgan Korusu Parkı

Rumeli Hisarı

Fatih Sultan Mehmet Köprüsü

ETİLER

BEBEK

ARNAVUTKÖY

KURUÇEŞME

BEŞİKTAŞ

ORTAKÖY

YILDIZ

Boğaziçi

Boğaziçi

Boğaziçi

Boğaziçi

Boğaziçi

Çırağan Sarayı

Dolmabahçe Sarayı

Bebek Parkı

Approximate scale

1 kilometre

½ mile

A stay in Istanbul isn't complete without a stroll along the shore or a boat trip up the tranquil waters of the Bosphorus, a 32-kilometre-long winding strait, which separates Europe from Asia and joins the Sea of Marmara to the Black Sea. Whether you prefer your viewing experience at ground or sea level, the view is guaranteed to be breathtaking.

The ancient Greeks coined the term 'bosphorus', meaning 'the strait of the cow', in reference to one of Zeus's romantic conquests, Io, who was turned into a cow by a jealous Hera. Chased by a bee sent by Hera to torment her, the path Io ran along became known as the Bosphorus. Today the past mingles with the present in perfect harmony along the shores of this strategically important waterway, and visitors can trace a route, beginning with the 19th-century Dolmabahçe Sarayı (Dolmabahçe Palace), along its banks to include spectacular Ottoman residences, beautiful gardens, picturesque villages and forested parks. After an exhaustive tour of the palace – pausing to take in the chandelier given by Queen Victoria and the room in which Atatürk died – the five-star Çırağan Palace Hotel, another former royal residence, is a good spot at which to sip Turkish coffee whilst admiring the view. Opposite the hotel's entrance is the vast Yıldız Parkı, which contains yet more imperial buildings, including Yıldız Şale (p. 94).

Ortaköy, once the summer resort of sultans due to its attractive location, is one of the liveliest areas along the route, particularly on weekends when shoppers stop for brunch at the small cafés lining its cobbled streets, before hitting the local crafts market. Arnavutköy, with its crumbling wooden houses opening onto the Bosphorus, is probably the most picturesque district in the entire city, and boasts a superb concentration of fish restaurants. Bebek, the home of diplomats and foreign businessmen since the 1950s, is the neighbourhood of choice for those with money to spend. Today Bebek buzzes with new and trendy cafés, which jostle for space alongside established local shops and coffee-houses.

Further along the route, Rumeli Hisarı is the name of both the imposing fort built by Mehmet the Conqueror and the nearby village. Nestled around the fort's huge walls are small cafés serving Turkish-style breakfasts, including bitter coffee and the ubiquitous white cheese, accompanied by a fresh Bosphorus breeze. Further still is Tarabya, a little cove at the far end of the Bosphorus, where the fish is always fresh at the many restaurants lining its seaside promenade.

ALWAYS IN VOGUE

1 Vogue

MILK AND HONEY

2 Pando

THE FRENCH CHEF

3 La Maison

PALACE IN THE WOODS

4 Yıldız Parkı + Yıldız Şale

Palanga Caddesi 23

Occupying a hillside location overlooking the Bosphorus, Yıldız park was the favourite playground of the Ottoman sultans. Selim III built a mansion here in honour of his mother, and successive emperors added new facilities. Eventually, the entire complex became known as Yıldız Sarayı (Yıldız Palace) and served as the empire's fourth government headquarters. Part of the palace, Yıldız Şale (Yıldız Chalet) is one of the most striking examples of 19th-century Ottoman architecture in the city. Built as a guest house to accommodate foreign statesmen, there are sixty rooms and four grand halls. Among its treasures are delicate engravings, baroque furniture, doors inlaid with mother-of-pearl, and the Hereke carpet, made from a single piece of cloth (over 400 square metres) and the largest of its kind in the world.

HOT SPOT IN THE CITY

5 Feriye Lokantası

KOSHER FARE

6 Carne

Muallim Naci Caddesi 17A

Carne, located just a stone's throw from the local synagogue, is the only restaurant in Istanbul that specializes in Jewish cuisine. As such, it is closed on Shabbat and holy days and its menu strictly adheres to Jewish dietary guidelines. Guests will not notice the absence of shellfish, however, as they tuck into such dishes as *İspanyol Böreği* (pastry with minced meat and walnut), *hummus* and *falafel*. Interior designer Eren Yorulmazer has toned down his usual flamboyant style to produce a minimalist and relaxed interior. Reservations are strongly recommended.

LUNCH AT THE MARKET

7 Sedir

Mecidiye Köprüsü Sokak 16-18

With its street market and young crowd, Ortaköy is reminiscent of London's Covent Garden. But although the seaside location has the advantage over the original, when it comes to decent eateries, Istanbul's version suffers somewhat. The owners of Sedir stepped in to fill the gap in 2002, converting an historic Greek mansion into an all-day café with quality service. Created by design team Autoban (p. 27), Sedir's interior is warm and welcoming, as are the large portions of classic bistro food, and guests linger over coffee and thoughtfully scattered magazines. The liberal use of wood, brick and comfortable summer-house furniture is perfectly in keeping with the history of the property.

FALL IN LOVE

8 Aşşk Café

Muallim Naci Caddesi 170/IA

Confident that diners will fall in love with both the perfect location and the food, this seaside café takes its name from a slightly punctuated version of the Turkish word for love. The menu is based on a healthy, organic cuisine, with the result that the café is populated by fitness fanatics on their way to a workout at next door's Planet Health Club. Sunday brunch in the cobbled garden or on the seaside deck is a wonderful way to spend a sunny day, and the Aşşk Toast (cheese, herbs and tomato tucked between slices of Russian bread) is delicious. A large selection of coffee and freshly-squeezed juice is also on offer.

HANDLE WITH CARE

9 İznik Foundation

LIVE MUSIC

10 Ece Aynalı Meyhane

Tramvay Caddesi 104

A lively *meyhane* is located on the ground floor of this venue, and above it is a restaurant-bar, both offering live music. Owner Ece Aksoy serves classic Aegean fare on a large scale. The dishes vary from Seferad cuisine to the flavours of Central Anatolia, all with a strong olive oil base. But it is the yellow vodka that makes Ece Aynalı Meyhane such a popular place with Istanbul's literati. The recipe is a closely guarded secret, but we did notice a trace of lemon!

11 Yedi Sekiz Hasan Paşa

Şehit Asım Caddesi 12

Located in Beşiktaş, one of the oldest and most colourful districts in Istanbul, the bakery Yedi Sekiz Hasan Paşa also boasts an unusual name. The phrase has particular significance to the district, as Hasan Paşa was the policeman who suppressed a rebellion against Sultan Adülhamid II. He was also an illiterate man, and his signature was a combination of the numbers seven (*yedi*) and eight (*sekiz*), thus forming the name by which he was always known. Incorporating an historic furnace at its centre, and an equally ancient marble-top display counter, Yedi Sekiz Hasan Paşa offers the best cookies (particularly the orange-flavoured ones) in town.

CAKE COUTURE

12 Café di Dolce

Kuruçeşme Caddesi 25

When it comes to flowers and cakes, everyone's favourite name in the city is Nilgün Ertuğ. After starting her small flower shop Nature in 1984, Ertuğ decided to pursue her other hobby of designing cakes. Thus Dolce, famous for its party cakes, was born. Not content with providing Istanbul's best-loved flowers and treats, Ertuğ also channelled her inner Martha Stewart and became the ultimate wedding organizer. In addition to its cakes and generous breakfasts, Café di Dolce serves up delicious brownies and macaroons. Baguettes and Indian *chipatis* can be found at the next-door bakery, and a recently-added stand serves traditional *köfte-ekmek* (meatballs between bread, the Turkish equivalent of a hamburger).

MEATBALLS ARE US

13 Ali Baba Köftecisi

1. Cadde 104

Arnavutköy might be known for its fish restaurants, but a few other addresses are worth a visit, and Ali Baba Köftecisi is one of them. Of its two venues located in the same street, one is small, with barely enough room for its four tables, and the other is more spacious, providing seating over two floors. On the rather sparse menu are meatballs, *piyaz* (a side-dish of dried beans cooked in olive oil), and a few traditional desserts. Despite the paucity of the menu, the tables at Ali Baba are never vacant, from lunchtime through to the later hours of the evening.

TIME FOR BREAKFAST

14 Bahar Pastanesi

1. Cadde 46

When the sun is shining and the weather is fine, a favourite Istanbul pastime is to start the day with the full monty at Bahar. Diners can either opt for the traditional Turkish breakfast of fried eggs, olives, white cheese and jam, or choose from the fresh pastries displayed on the vast counter. The only difficulty is finding a vacant table. Should you be successful, prepare to eat your breakfast under the beady gaze of hungry diners waiting (rather less than patiently) in the long queue. Bahar also has a branch on Kınalıada (p. 178).

POPULAR ARTISTS

15 PG Art Gallery

Cevdet Paşa Caddesi 386/2-3

After two years as a former consultant at the well-known Vakko Art Gallery, Pırıl Güleşçi opened her own gallery in 1993. The PG Art Gallery focuses on exhibiting the works of popular local and national contemporary artists, and each year stages six painting exhibitions, along with exhibitions highlighting photography and sculpture. The gallery is closed on Mondays.

NEIGHBOURHOOD BAR

16 Lucca

Cevdet Paşa Caddesi 51/B

The pressing need for a café-bar in the neighbourhood, together with its philosophy of catering to the the global need for comfort food, guaranteed the overwhelming success of Lucca. Open eighteen hours a day, Lucca is a great place for a full breakfast while reading the newspaper, or a quick latte on the way home. At night, the bar buzzes with thirty-somethings and loud music. The venue was formerly home to Bebek Lokal (a popular meeting place in the 1960s), and the original ceiling decorations have been carefully restored. Try to stop by on 'Cleaning Day', a sort of car-boot sale held on the the last Saturday of every month.

GOD BLESS CANDIES!

17 Bebek Badem Ezmecisi

Cevdet Paşa Caddesi 238/1

A Bebek classic, this small shop has specialized in almond marzipan for the last hundred years. Mehmet Halil İşgüder opened his first store in 1904, and today it is run by his daughter, Sevim. Bebek Badem Ezmecisi's delicious sweets are still produced with İşgüder's traditional (and secret) formula. There are also cookies and candies, displayed in Beykoz glass jars. Pictures of the founders hang proudly on the wall, and, rather charmingly, a board proclaiming 'Yaşasın Şeker!' (God bless candies!) welcomes you upon entering the store.

BOSPHORUS CLASSIC

18 Bebek Bar

155

COMFORT FOOD

19 Mangerie

Cevdet Paşa Caddesi 69/3

Mangerie's self-educated chef Elif Yalın Topkaya is also the host of a weekly television cookery programme and a former partner of The House Café (p. 149). Together with Lucca (see this page), Mangerie is one of the many recently-opened cafés in Bebek, injecting fresh life into the neighbourhood. Although discreetly tucked away on the third floor of an apartment building, the restaurant is always crowded with Istanbul's hip and fashionable. The massive tables are comfortably placed, and the mismatched furniture (think Eames chair next to a flea-market sofa) and industrial open-plan kitchen create a perfect accompaniment to perfect dishes. On warmer days, a wide veranda provides a more relaxed eating environment, and guests lounging on the sunbeds will find their eggs Benedict brought to them on a tea-tray.

BURGERS IN BEBEK

20 Ab'bas

Cevdet Paşa Caddesi 177

Istanbul has many late night, fast-food joints, particularly in the heart of its nightlife area, Taksim. Ab'bas is located in Bebek, a somewhat less lively area, yet it is the oldest of its kind within the district and is always crowded, no matter what time of day. Justly famous for its legendary Ab'bas Burger (a hamburger made from skewered meat and cooked over charcoal) and the Bebek Burger (cheeseburger with eggs), Ab'bas stays open until 5 a.m. The recent addition of a waffle stand has only added to Ab'bas's popularity, but the true regular knows that the real attraction here is the burgers.

21 Bebek Parkı + Bebek Kahve

Cevdet Paşa Caddesi 13

One of the most historic districts along the Bosphorus, Bebek has always been a symbol of wealth. After elegant villas began to appear in the 18th century, Bebek park was built as a public space to provide a little greenery amidst all the luxuriousness. Today, the district still preserves some of its historic charm, though many of the houses have been replaced by apartment buildings, and enormous yachts now line the seaside promenade. Nearby Turkish coffee house, Bebek Kahve, is a favourite meeting spot for Bebek's youth, who arrive for home-made apple pie over a game (or several) of backgammon.

LIKE AN EXTRA VIRGIN
22 Laleli Zeytinyağları

Cevdet Paşa Caddesi 97/A

Despite being a Mediterranean speciality for the last 8,000 years and the basis of Ottoman cuisine, shops specializing in olive oil are somewhat of a new phenomenon in Turkey. But a few are to be found, including the small, family-run Laleli Zeytinyağları, which produces its own oils at its facilities in Midilli. Its shelves are filled with different varieties of olive oil (try the garlic) and olive-based products such as soap. Many of the world's most popular brands of olive oil are in fact Turkish, and are repackaged with Italian names. Feel free to taste the many oils on offer.

EQUESTRIAN VILLA
23 Sakıp Sabancı Müzesi

İstinye Caddesi 22

One of Turkey's wealthiest families, the Sabancıs amassed a stupendous collection of 15th- to 20th-century Ottoman calligraphy, today internationally recognized as the most prestigious collection of its kind. Their historic villa, with its bronze horse at the entrance overlooking the Bosphorus, has been turned into a museum to showcase the manuscript collection, along with porcelain and Turkish paintings. The museum also hosts various national and international exhibitions throughout the year, and recently held *Three Centuries of European Fashion* from the collection of fashion historian, Alexandre Vassiliev.

TURKISH-STYLE CAFÉ

24 Sade Kahve
Yahya Kemal Caddesi 36

Occupying the first two floors of an old wooden house, Sade
Kahve is a captivating Turkish-style coffee-house on the
shore of the Bosphorus. With its wooden chairs and floral
tablecloths, and highly unusual accessories (including a
large arts-and-crafts wooden spoon perched next to a hi-fi
speaker) adorning every inch of its walls, the ground-
floor café is an ideal setting for breakfast with a sea breeze.
The upstairs restaurant is more restrained, with marble
floors and bookshelves stuffed with vintage accessories.
Even in winter diners are gently encouraged to sit outside,
and provided with shawls and charcoal braziers for cold
shoulders and toes.

PIER-LESS DINING

25 İskele
İskele Meydanı 4/1

It's hard to imagine a better setting in which to enjoy a
seafood supper than İskele. Hovering above the sea, the
restaurant perches on top of the old ferry pier, built during
the Ottoman Empire, near the Rumeli Hisarı fortress.
After serving its original purpose for decades, the pier
was leased in 1991 to private individuals who have carefully
restored its architectural features. Despite recent
extensions to increase seating capacity, the historic
structure still maintains its original appearance, at least
from the roadside.

GREEN IS NOT THE ONLY COLOUR

26 Emirgan Korusu
Emirgan Korusu Caddesi

Perfectly situated in a picturesque location on the
Bosphorus, this vast park, famous for its tulip gardens,
contains three historic pavilions. Restored to its original
condition is the Yellow Pavilion, which functions as an á
là carte restaurant during the week and serves buffet
brunches on weekends. Also offering refreshment is the
Pink Pavilion, which serves tea from a samovar. The
neoclassical White Pavilion, the largest of the lot, is not
open to the public. Emirgan Korusu's last owner, arms
dealer Lütfi Tozan, handed the park over to the
government in the 1930s.

27 Zeynel

Köybaşı Caddesi 144

Natives agree that when it comes to ice cream, Zeynel is where it's at. Founder Zeynel Bölükbaşı began his small business in 1925 by delivering home-made ice cream to the Bosphorus's waterside mansions in his rowboat. The delivery service came to an end in 1948, but the family business continues to produce and serve thirteen varieties of its legendary ice cream (along with two diet versions), as well as a selection of desserts, including *kazandibi* (bottom-of-the-pot) rice pudding and *aşure*, which contains around twenty ingredients and is traditionally believed to have been the last meal on Noah's Ark.

28 Emek 2 Kahve

Daire Sokak

Sandwiched between Yeniköy's opulent houses, this unpretentious seaside café is one of the most popular in the neighbourhood and is always crowded. A perfect place for lazy Sunday breakfasts, Emek 2 Kahve serves up *menemen* (eggs baked with tomatoes, green peppers and cheese) and hot or cold sandwiches, as well as toast. The menus themselves are tucked between magazine covers from the 1960s. On sunny days, only the fortunate will find a vacant outside table. Inside is a gloomier prospect, with lots of dark wooden furniture, but it is difficult to find a table in there, too.

29 Kıyı

140

30 Meşhur Kireçburnu Fırını

Kireçburnu Caddesi 21

Local residents call Meşhur Kireçburnu Fırını 'the best pastry shop on earth,' and after tasting its legendary *kıymalı börek* (savoury pastry with mince and currants), it's hard to disagree. A few tables are available for those who want to savour their purchases on site, but we recommend getting your pastry to go for munching while sauntering along the Bosphorus.

Asian Side

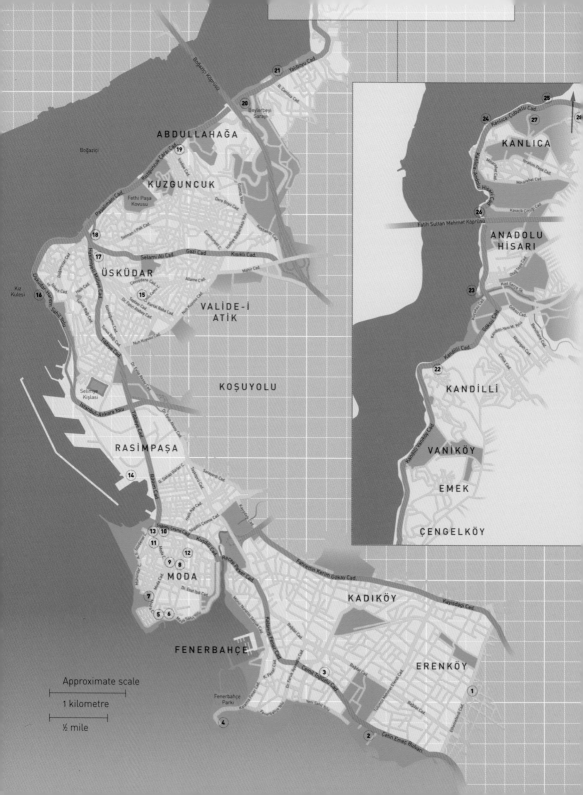

Less touristy and more residential than its European counterpart with quiet and affluent neighbourhoods lining the coast, Istanbul's Asian side offers a totally different experience to that found in the districts of the opposite shore. Although many first-timers expect to find an atmosphere more redolent of the Orient (it is Asia, after all), ironically, it is this part of the city that is filled with sprawling Western-style suburbs.

Drawing near to Kadıköy Port, visitors arriving by ferry (the best way to reach and appreciate this part of the city) are welcomed by the magnificent Haydarpaşa railway station (p. 112). This is where both the Baghdad Railway and the Asian shore begin. The Anatolian suburb of Kadıköy (formerly Chaldecon, and older than Byzantium) is to the Asian side what Taksim is to the European quarter, even boasting its own historic tram. The centre of business, shopping and entertainment, Kadıköy's streets are endlessly buzzing with activity, whereas nearby Moda, one of the wealthier districts in this part of Istanbul, is calm and peaceful. Bağdat Caddesi, the avenue of chic boutiques and cafés, is where the area's bright young things gather to show off their trendy clothes and expensive cars. Clustered between the districts of Suadiye and Erenköy at the street's southern end, the cafés are often full to bursting, spilling out onto the pavement on sunny days.

Further north along the Asian coast of the Bosphorus is the conservative district of Üsküdar, known by the Greeks as Chrysopolis, or the 'city of gold'. Traditionally thought to have been founded in 686 BC, Üsküdar was the point from which the Roman Empire's roads stretched east into Asia. Among Üsküdar's many mosques, of particular interest are two of royal architect Mimar Sinan's creations, the tiny Şemsi Ahmet Paşa Camii and the much larger Atik Valide Camii (p. 112). Nearby is Beylerbeyi Sarayı (p. 115), built at the end of the 19th century by court architect Sarkis Balyan and home of the deposed Sultan Abdülhamit II.

Venturing north along the shore, beyond Üsküdar, are two unspoiled waterside villages, Çengelköy, famed for both the tiny cucumbers sold from its many street-vendor carts and for featuring in a popular television soap, and Kanlıca, itself famous since at least the 17th century for its yoghurt. Along with these historic sites and charming villages, the Asian side is lined with luxurious villas, ferociously guarded behind high walls, whose architectural beauty is best seen from the water.

1 Ethemefendi 36
Ethemefendi Caddesi 36

Overshadowed by hundred-year-old chestnut trees, this 20th-century chalet now operates as a restaurant and gift store, and is one of the best-kept secrets of the Asian side. Once owned by a former governor of Egypt, the house has been extensively renovated, but has managed to retain its former grandeur. The menu is divided into sections; *meze* are found under 'Rendezvous with Rakı'. Along with fish, Ethemefendi 36 also serves a wide variety of meat dishes. Unusual names are a feature of the menu, and the dessert *zegna* takes its name from its ingredients (fig and walnut), while the sea bass with spinach is called 'mermaid'.

OUT OF AFRICA
2 Café Zanzibar

145

SWEET DREAMS
3 Cemilzade
Cemil Topuzlu Caddesi 7/4

Opened in 1883, the confectionery Cemilzade is famous for its *lokums* and pistachio marzipan. Founder Udi Cemil Bey was a musician (with a particular fondness for the lute), and his musical career dictated Cemilzade's geographical journey. Invited to Egypt to teach music to the imperial court, Cemil Bey set up a sweetshop in Cairo. After twenty years and the death of its founder, the shop returned to Istanbul, eventually settling on this site. Two more branches followed. The many varieties of marzipan, colourful boiled sweets in glass jars, and trays of *lokum* look as enticingly delicious as they taste.

TEA AND FOOTIE
4 Fenerbahçe Parkı
Fenerbahçe Parkı

Despite having a name more associated with football than leafy tranquility, Fenerbahçe Parkı (*fener* means lighthouse, and *bahçe* is garden) is the most beautiful park on the Asian side. A delight for dogs and joggers alike, Fenerbahçe's tea gardens are never short of customers. Although it can quickly turn into an overcrowded nightmare during sunny weekends, the park is ideal for tea with *simit* on weekday mornings. On Sundays, the park heaves with visitors tucking into home-made jam, fresh eggs and tea served (of course) in tulip-shaped glasses.

ON A FISH AND A PRAYER
5 Koço Restaurant
Moda Caddesi 265

At the point where Moda's main street meets the Sea of Marmara lies Koço, one of Istanbul's most unusual fish restaurants. With its creaky wooden floors, vivid blue tablecloths, and menu of fish, *meze* and *rakı*, Koço offers everything one would expect from a decent fish restaurant. Its unusual character is apparent at the bottom of the short flight of stairs to the basement, where, most unexpectedly, is the ancient Greek church of St Ekaterini, unearthed while digging the restaurant's foundations. Today, visitors desiring to light a candle and offer a prayer in the church have to pass through the restaurant. Assuming that their prayers will be answered (the church has a reputation for good results!), they return through the restaurant for a celebration over good fish and wine.

PIZZA MY HEART
6 Moda Teras
Moda Mektebi Sokak 7/9

Located on a hilltop long favoured as the summer resort of choice for Istanbul's wealthy, Moda Teras is a restaurant-bar designed by Autoban (p. 27). Lavish attention to detail is visible everywhere, including the twinkling fairy-lights in the trees of the beautifully landscaped garden terrace. The highlight of the menu is the recent (and vastly popular) addition of thin and crispy pizzas baked in the restaurant's wood-burning oven. Old-fashioned favourites are also on offer, including sea bass in a basket, and *hünkar rüyası* (grilled fillet medallions on aubergine mash). During the evening hours, the action continues in the large and achingly trendy bar.

ORCHID ICE CREAM
7 Ali Usta
Moda Caddesi 264/A

Around thirty flavours of ice cream, including mint, almond, walnut, pistachio and the popular Santa Maria, along with four diet varieties, are on offer at this tiny shop located in the fashionable neighbourhood of Moda. Famous for its ice cream made from *salep* (a whitish flour milled from the dried tubers of wild orchids), Ali Usta has been the premier glacier in the area since 1968. Long queues form in front of the stand all year long, but just one bite is enough to realize the wait was worth it.

8 6:45

Kadife Sokak 21

6:45 calls its inventory 'life's surprising objects,' and its shelves live up to the claim, containing books, comics, music-related items, pencils, herbal teas, second-hand walking sticks and sculptures labelled 'from the garbageman Deniz'. Originally in the publishing business, the founders of 6:45 decided to set up a bookshop with reasonable prices, and to add an element of fun to the proceedings. The result is a small shop of oddities that deserves a visit, whether it is a book or an old shaving set that you have in mind.

CULTURE AND COCKTAILS

9 Karga(rt)

Kadife Sokak 16

In contrast to the European side of the city, the Asian shore has traditionally been lacking in the nightlife department. Karga, the exception to the rule, has become a magnet for the area's youthful crowd since opening its doors in 1996, serving up both good music and modern art. Set in one of four houses built to accommodate builders working at the Haydarpaşa train station construction site (p. 112), Karga operates as a café-bar on the first two floors, and as a centre of culture and art on the top two, holding exhibitions, showing films and documentaries, and hosting theatre and modern dance events.

OLDER THAN THE REPUBLIC

10 Yanyalı Fehmi Lokantası

Yağlıkçı İsmail Sokak 1

Yanyalı Fehmi Lokantası has been serving traditional Turkish cuisine since the 1920s to its devoted fans, including İsmet İnönü, the second president of the Turkish Republic. Originally from Yanya (Ionnina), in Greece, founder Fehmi Bey (who later took the name Sönmezler) went into the restaurant business upon meeting a retired palace cook. Now run by younger generations of Sönmezlers, the two-storey restaurant still serves such popular dishes as *Acem Tavuğu* (chicken and rice, wrapped in an omelette) and *Paşa Kebabı* (beef with aubergine, mushrooms and cheese). Waiting diners can keep a hungry eye on proceedings in the visible kitchen.

11 Çiya

Güneşli Bahçe Sokak 43–44–48/B

Located at the far end of the Kadıköy fish market, such is Çiya's popularity that it has expanded into several properties (including Çiya Sofrası and Çiya Kebapçı), all facing each other in the same street. Çiya serves around 100 different types of kebap, and a vast variety of dishes from Southeastern Anatolia and the Eastern Mediterranean. The determined efforts of owner Musa Dağdeviren to widen the répertoire of Turkish cuisine has led to the menu's startling variety. Whether you choose a kebap or a rice dish (of which there are around forty varieties), be sure to finish off your meal with *mırra*, a local coffee from the south east.

A CULTURAL HERITAGE

12 Süreyya Sineması

Bahariye Caddesi 29

Opening in 1927, Süreyya Sineması was the first venue in Istanbul to host Turkish operettas. The building liberally borrowed architectural elements from other structures in Europe, even ordering a European lighting and heating system despite the fact that electricity was not yet available in the city. In 1930 the opera house became a popular cinema, and after a refurbishment in 1994, today Süreyya Sineması offers Hollywood blockbusters in a stunning and historic setting. Not all of the original features have been so carefully preserved, however: the former ballroom is now a department store, and the open-air cinema has been converted into a carpark.

OLD-FASHIONED PATISSERIE

13 Baylan Pastanesi

155

READY FOR DEPARTURE

14 Haydarpaşa Tren İstasyonu

İstasyon Caddesi

Overlooking Kadıköy Bay, the Haydarpaşa train station breathes a little old-world glamour into this excessively developed area. This splendid railway station was a present to the Sultan and people of Istanbul from Kaiser Wilhelm II, and was built by two of his compatriots, Otto Ritter and Helmut Cuno, in 1906. The neoclassical building's sandstone façade leads into an interior festooned with trailing garlands and lit by stained glass windows. Despite the station's somewhat sad subsequent history – soldiers boarded trains here for the front in the First World War – its opulent beauty is certainly testament to Kaiser Wilhelm's spectacular taste in presents.

MOSQUE OF AGES

15 Atik Valide Camii

Çinili Camii Sokak

Designed by Sinan in 1583 for the mother of Sultan Murad III, this beautiful mosque showcases one of the finest examples of tiling decoration in the city. With its window shutters inlaid with mother-of-pearl and ivory, and exquisite panels depicting blossoming plum branches on either side of its *mihrab* niche, Atik Valide Camii is a true work of art. Built on a slope, the hexagonal mosque is also notable for its unique layout, as the main structure and the outbuildings are situated on different levels. Unfortunately, the mosque has been seriously neglected in recent years, and its lead domes have been targeted by thieves. However, like all of Sinan's great works, the mosque has managed to stand against the ravages of time.

FISH AND THE MAIDEN

16 Arab'ın Yeri

İskele Caddesi 18

Tiny hilltop district Salacak oozes cosiness from every pore, and one of its star attractions, Arab'ın Yeri (also known as Huzur Restaurant), is among the oldest seafood venues in the area. Although there are some new and stylish arrivals (Deniz and Angel are two such newcomers), this old neighbourhood establishment with its picture-postcard view of Kız Kulesi (Maiden's Tower) is still a favourite. Of course, the expensive cars outside don't arrive here just for the view: the fish is fresh and fabulous, and the varieties of *meze* are endless.

TO MARKET, TO MARKET

17 Üsküdar Bitpazarı

Büyükhamam Sokak

The century-old Üsküdar Bitpazarı is the premier antiques bazaar of Istanbul and home to a large number of dealers. A veritable maze of treasures and bargain prices, the bazaar sells an exhaustive range of goods, from Anatolian wooden doors to sets of Ottoman china. As with all markets – from Üsküdar to Petticoat Lane – the earlier you arrive, the better. Occupying the two basement floors of a huge building, this bazaar is not the most aesthetically pleasing, but is a must for anyone's visit to the city.

suna'nın yeri

DİL   : 15. YTL
TEKİR   : 15
ÇİNEKOP : 15
MEZGİT   : 15
LEVREK   : 10
ÇUPRA   : 10

18 Kanaat Lokantası

HOME COOKING
19 Asude Ev Yemekleri
Perihan Abla Sokak 4

Heading north up the coast, Kuzguncuk is the first village on the Asian side, set in a peaceful wooded valley overlooking the rippling waters of the Bosphorus. Amongst its spectacular wooden houses there are some decent eateries, and fish restaurant İsmet Baba is one of them. But since the city is overloaded with fishy fare, head to Perihan Abla Sokak (named after the TV series of the same name filmed in the area) and have a seat at one of the four tables at Asude Ev Yemekleri, which serves hearty dishes (*mantı* on Saturdays) in a cheerful, friendly setting.

A ROYAL SUMMER HOUSE
20 Beylerbeyi Sarayı
Abdullahağa Caddesi

Of all the residences of the Ottoman Sultans, only Beylerbeyi Sarayı gives the impression of having once been lived in. Designed by Sarkis Balyan during the reign of Sultan Abdülaziz, Beylerbeyi was primarily used as a summer house, and to accommodate foreign heads of state, including Empress Eugénie of France. Consisting of two main floors and a basement to house the kitchens and storage rooms, the exterior façade (sporting carved garlands of fig and quince) of this architectural gem is in the Ottoman neoclassical style. Inside are twenty-six chambers and six grand halls, and the Inlaid Pearl Room contains a chair carved by Abdülaziz himself. The terraced gardens on the sloping hillside behind the palace are connected to the main building by a tunnel which now acts as a sales desk.

THE NAME SAYS IT ALL
21 Bosphorus Palace Hotel

128

FISH AHOY!
22 Suna'nın Yeri
İskele Caddesi 4

Suna Türksever, the owner of this modest seafood restaurant, has dedicated her life to serving only the best to her customers. When she set up Suna'nın Yeri some thirty years ago, she realized that after the expense of renovation there was no money left over for crockery. Undeterred, Türksever brought a set of dishes from her own home and started business. Focusing on fish, only the freshest will do, a rule which explains why Suna'nın Yeri is packed with gourmands from all over the city. On warmer days, tables spill over into the tiny garden in between the restaurant's two buildings. *Rakı* (the local tipple made from aniseed spirit and similar to pastis) arrives in a coffee cup because of the restaurant's proximity to a mosque.

ECLECTIC GRANDEUR
23 Küçüksu Kasrı
Küçüksu Çayırı Sahili

A two-storey wooden house formerly stood on this shoreside location, where the Göksu river meets the Bosphorus (a point more commonly known as the *Eaux Douces d'Asie*, or the Sweet Waters of Asia). However, during the reign of Sultan Abdülmecid in the first half of the 19th century, the old building was replaced by a stone palace designed by royal architect Nikogos Balyan, which now functions as a museum. In contrast to other imperial palaces, Küçüksu Kasrı is not surrounded by high walls, but rather by iron railings with gates opening in all four directions. Inside are Italian marble fireplaces in various shapes and colours, gracious plaster reliefs, a baroque staircase, delicate parquetry and a stunning collection of carpets and paintings.

QUALITY TRANQUILITY
24 A'jia

MUSIC FOR THE MASSES
25 Hayal Kahvesi
Burunbahçe Mevkii

Hayal Kahvesi fulfils the important function of supporting national rock and jazz groups. Situated in a stone warehouse on the shore with a decking area in front, over the last ten years this large and airy venue has become a summer staple for Istanbul's music lovers. With concerts by local and international performers, and live DJs behind the decks, there is always a carnival-like atmosphere raging within the premises. Hayal Kahvesi can be reached by sea, taking the boat from İstinye, although after a few drinks the return trip might not be so appealing.

UNDER THE BRIDGE

26 Lacivert

Körfez Caddesi 57/A

Located right underneath the Fatih Sultan Mehmet Koprüsü (bridge), Lacivert couldn't be easier to find. For those less map-savvy diners, the restaurant's boat picks up guests from the European side bringing them to this Asian shore treasure. Lacivert's two rooms and outdoor terrace have views of the Rumeli Hisarı fortress, majestically rising from the opposite shore. The menu is skillful and rich, offering such hearty Mediterranean fare as grilled salmon on mashed potato, and veal *carpaccio* with artichoke leaves. The very good wine list stocks a large selection of Turkish wines, as well as the usual imports.

AMONG THE WOODS AND ROSE PETALS

27 Hıdiv Kasrı

Çubuklu Hıdiv Yolu 32

Perfectly situated in the serene atmosphere of the Küçük Çamlıca woods, Hıdiv Kasrı (Hıdiv Pavilion), with its world-famous rose gardens, has a stunning view of the Bosphorus. Its tower is reached by the first-ever steam-powered lift (unfortunately not open to public). *Hıdiv* was the title given by the sultans to governors of the Egyptian province, and this pavilion was once the residence of Abbas Hilmi Paşa, the last governor, who also built a twin version on the banks of the River Nile. Recently restored, Hıdiv Kasrı now acts as a restaurant serving Turkish cuisine, and the weekend buffet is popular with locals.

A SHRINE ON THE HILL

28 Yuşa Tepesi

Yuşa Tepesi Yolu

Located on the highest hill of the Asian side, the site of this enormous mausoleum (12 metres in length) has been revered as a holy place since ancient times. The grave is traditionally believed to have been that of the prophet Yuşa, who, according to the Old Testament, was the apprentice of Moses. Faithful flocking to the site today present votive offerings in the hopes of purifying their souls. Pilgrims and visitors alike can revel in the mesmerizing views from the hill, and can satisfy their hunger pangs in nearby Anadolu Kavağı, famed for its many seafood restaurants.

sleep

There is a room for every style taste in Istanbul, and weary guests, from design addicts to devotees of five-star luxury, are sure to find the hotel of their dreams. For those who like a little pampering with their room service, suitable suites offering the royal treatment can be found at the illustrious grande-dame hotels lining the Taksim-Nişantaşı route. Boutique hotels, with their quirky charm and Ottoman décor, are dotted throughout the city. Whatever option travellers choose, each hotel provides old-world hospitality in the midst of an ever-changing city.

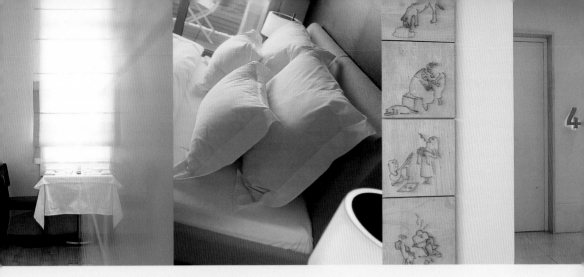

4

QUALITY TRANQUILITY

 A'jia

24 Kanlıca-Çubuklu Caddesi 27
Rooms from €250

With dramatic views of the Bosphorus from the tranquil shores of Kanlıca, A'jia (the Japanese word for Asia), is a unique and elegant 16-room hotel that takes care that each guest without exception receives the VIP treatment. The original building was once the home of Ottoman governor Ahmet Rasim Paşa, and until 1970 had been used as a school. Revamped by architect Reşit Soley and managed by the ubiquitous Istanbul Doors Group (see p. 158 for Vogue and p. 84 for Da Mario), the new-look A'jia has injected fresh life into the Asian side of the city.

The sophisticated interior, dominated by modern furniture, contemporary art and an all-white colour scheme, is a perfect contrast to the historic exterior. Each room is equipped with a king-sized bed (with equally large and invitingly fluffy goose-down pillows), air conditioning, a personal safe and wireless Internet access. Even the bathrooms provide luxuries for weary guests, and include a robe and slippers. Five of the ten double-rooms have a private balcony, three of the six suites have mezzanine floors, and almost all of the rooms, both double and deluxe, look directly onto the Bosphorus. The hotel is accessible by sea, but valet parking is also available for less adventurous travellers.

The minimal sophistication employed by Soley for the interior is extended to the superb restaurant, which offers Mediterranean cuisine prepared by award-winning Turkish chef, Mustafa Baylan. During the summer months, the banqueting facilities on the terrace can seat up to 300 diners, or host up to 600 cocktail party guests, to the background accompaniment of music and the engines of passing fishing boats.

14

30

Ansen 130

Meşrutiyet Caddesi 130

Rooms from €205

A welcome new addition to Istanbul's roster of hotels, Ansen 130 is a boutique hotel located in the Tünel area, and offers historic architectural elegance with a touch of modern comfort. This small hotel, consisting of just ten suites, is located just a stone's throw from the city's best restaurants and bars. If you are fortunate enough to have secured a suite on one of the top floors (try to get suite 501), your private view is the breathtaking sunset over the Golden Horn.

The name Ansen 130 derives from a combination of the 150-year-old apartment building's original name (Ansen was the surname of the family that owned the building) and its street number. The old signboard has been kept in memory of its past owners and now adorns the wall behind the bar. Sympathetically converted by Yılmaz Değer, also the architect behind the building project for the country's leading GSM company, the historic façade has been retained. Conference facilities are fully-equipped with dataports and Internet access, and catering for up to eighty people is provided by ProLonge.

Ansen 130 is not the kind of hotel that intimidates visitors with an austere and formal lobby. Upon entrance, guests immediately find themselves in the middle of a chic café-bar surrounded by wood-panelled walls and local barflies. Just a few steps more brings travellers to Restaurant 130, which offers seating for thirty and cuisine which the hotel calls a 'fusion of New World and Mediterranean cuisine' under the guidance of renowned chef Mike Norman. Ansen Wine House next door provides cigars along with international vintages.

COMFORT IN SIMPLICITY

66 **Bentley Hotel**

6 Halaskargazi Caddesi 75
Rooms from €200

A member of the Design Hotels Group, the Bentley Hotel is one of Istanbul's top-end hotels. Opening in January 2003, its downtown location at the crossroads of Harbiye and Nişantaşı, within walking distance to the neighbourhood's eclectic shopping scene and such cultural destinations as Harbiye Askeri Müsezi (p. 68), contributed to the hotel's immediate popularity with both tourists and business travellers looking for a little gracious hospitality in their temporary homes.

The Bentley's interior was designed by Milanese duo Piero Lissoni and Nicoletta Canesi, who combined contemporary sophistication with eastern flair in every detail. The forty rooms and ten suites are large, airy and bright, and decorated in a harmonious blend of grey, brown and white. The hotel has thought of every eventuality, and has provided each suite with a phone line, two Internet lines, a CD collection and sound-system, and even an espresso machine. The two rooftop suites have their own terraces with terrific views of the Bosphorus and the Golden Horn for private sunbathing, and one of the suites includes an extra room for staff. For the more physically inclined, there is a fitness room and sauna in the basement.

Just like the décor, the food offered in the Bentley's first-floor restaurant is modern international embellished with a little Turkish flavour. The popular bar on the same floor is a good place for a pre-dinner drink prior to a slap-up meal at one of Nişantaşı 's trendy restaurants.

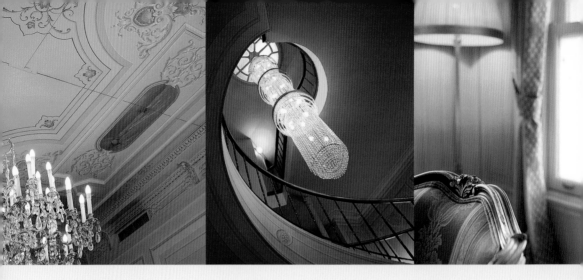

 Bosphorus Palace Hotel

 Yalıboyu Caddesi 64

Rooms from €160

The Bosphorus Palace Hotel is just what says on the tin: an historic palace converted into a boutique hotel, located on the shore of the Bosphorus. The site was once occupied by the home of Grand Vizier Damat Melek Mehmet Paşa, later replaced in 1890 by another house designed by Alexander Vallaury. Later still, the property was bought by İsmail Hakkı Paşa, a governor during the reign of Abdülhamit II. Damaged by fire in 1983, the building was carefully restored at the behest of the Ministry of Tourism, using old drawings and photographs to recreate as much as possible its original appearance.

The hotel has 14 rooms, each decorated in the classic Ottoman style with opulent details, such as gilded bedframes and mirrors. Even the antique furniture has been carefully sourced at auctions to reflect the house's past grandeur. The beautiful decoration on the ceilings are the work of the same craftsman who decorated the ceilings of the Dolmabahçe Palace. Modern amenities have not been forgotten amongst all this historical detail, and everything the business traveller or international jet-setter might require has been provided, from the personal room safe and mini-bar, to the dressing-gown and morning paper. The Godfather of Soul and, fittingly, the original James Bond have both stayed at the Bosphorus Palace Hotel.

The downstairs restaurant was a boathouse in its previous life, and offers a romantic seaside setting for a meal. It can accommodate wedding receptions and conferences for parties of up to 100 guests.

30 **Hotel Daphnis**

24 Sadrazam Ali Paşa Caddesi 26
Rooms from €70

Once through the door of this charming hotel, guests feel as if they are stepping (on creaky wooden floors) into the past. Formed by joining four adjacent 19th-century Greek villas, Hotel Daphnis, a self-described 108-year-old rum house, is a special class of hotel. Located in Fener, near Sultanahmet and across the Golden Horn from Karaköy and Beyoğlu, one side overlooks the water, while the other opens onto the historic İncebel Sokak, opposite the Greek Orthodox Patriarchate. A few doors down in the same street as the hotel is the little church of legends, Panaghia Mouchliotissa (p. 46).

Architect and owner Defne Yanger has renovated the hotel's 16 rooms (three suites and 13 double-rooms), while retaining the building's former appearance, preserving the hand-painted decorative figures (*kalemişler*) on the walls and the high wooden doors. The old gramophone in the lobby adds more nostalgia to the atmosphere, as do the stained-glass windows, marble sinks and old water pumps.

In the basement, Café Daphnis can seat 75 diners (40 inside and 35 in the flower-filled garden), and offers Greek cuisine accompanied by Mürefte wine. For breakfast, the Full Turkish (kashar cheese, olives, tomatoes, cucumbers, ham, honey and coffee) is available, and later diners can enjoy various pasta dishes, along with the more traditional Turkish favourites, *börek* (with eggplant and breadcrumbs) and *Tekirdağ* meatballs.

LOVELY AND AMAZING

30 **Hotel Empress Zoe**

15 Adliye Sokak 10
Rooms from €70

This tiny and friendly hotel is in the historic district of Sultanahmet, next to the ruins of the 15th-century İshak Paşa *hamam*, and offers more than just its 22 individually-decorated rooms. Opening twelve years ago, the hotel was converted from two old town houses, and takes its name from the Byzantine Empress Zoe, an intriguing character who ruled in her own right and married the first of several husbands at the age of fifty.

Today the Hotel Empress Zoe is a bargain hotel that doesn't skimp on charm. It is run by Ann Nevans, who treats the hotel very much as if it was her own home. She has created a minimal interior, consisting of primarily wood and stone, brought to life by the *kilims* and throws decorated with Özbek motifs scattered throughout. Each bathroom is decorated with marble or terracotta, and the penthouse and Chez Zoe suites are furnished with Turkish-style *hamam* bathrooms. The penthouse suite also comes with its own terrace overlooking the Sultanahmet Camii (Blue Mosque), and the Chez Garden suite offers a view of the beautiful palm-filled garden, in which can often be spotted a plump and gently snoring Jasper, the hotel's resident cat. Rooms are reached after navigating narrow corridors and the tiny spiral staircase, so travelling light is recommended.

The bar and breakfast area has Byzantine-style paintings on the walls, courtesy of Mrs Nevans's Greek brother-in-law, and the rooftop bar, housed within the split-level terrace, has lovely views of the Sea of Marmara, mosques and minarets.

30 İbrahim Paşa Hotel

12 Terzihane Sokak 5
Rooms from €125

Converted from a 19th-century four-storey townhouse, the İbrahim Paşa Hotel offers sophisticated and modern accommodation, a rarity in the Sultanahmet area, and is an ideal place to stay for first-time visitors wanting to explore Istanbul's historic monuments to their collective hearts' content. A large number of popular destinations, including the İbrahim Paşa Sarayı, which now houses the Türk ve İslam Eserleri Müzesi (p. 34), Hagia Sophia and the Topkapı Sarayı are within walking distance.

Upon entering the hotel, on the right is the lounge area, complete with fireplace, leather sofa and bookcase stuffed with night-time reading. A few steps further along is the light and inviting breakfast area, with its green walls hung with black and white family photographs. From the roof terrace, guests can feast their weary eyes on the spectacular domes of Sultanahmet Camii (Blue Mosque). Following a recent refurbishment, the 16 rooms are well equipped and comfortable (the four suites include a 'relaxation area'), and all are decorated in the ubiquitous contemporary-with-a-twist-of-Ottoman style. 24-hour room service and assistance with sorting out walking tours and concert tickets are also available.

After breakfast, the ground floor serves as a café-bar, where complimentary tea is served around the fireplace. The restrained atmosphere of the the İbrahim Paşa Hotel is as welcoming as owner Mehmet Umur's exuberant labrador, Godot.

ORIENTAL INTRIGUE

14 Pera Palas

22 Meşrutiyet Caddesi 98–100
Rooms from €180

A hotel that has seen the decline of an empire, the founding of a new republic and two World Wars has earned its place as one of Istanbul's most venerable landmarks, and Pera Palas, with its elegant façade, is one of the most recognizable structures in the city. Designed (again) by the remarkably busy Alexander Vallaury, it was built in 1891 to accommodate European passengers who arrived in Constantinople on the Orient Express. (For trivia fans, this is why the symbols of the hotel and the Orient Express are the same.)

The hotel's connections with the wealthy and famous began early (Sultan Abdülhamit attended the opening ceremony), and Pera Palas has made its name through its many famous returning regulars, including Sarah Bernhardt and Edward VIII. During her many visits between 1926 and 1932, Agatha Christie stayed in room 411, and wrote most of *Murder on the Orient Express* here. Christie famously went AWOL for eleven days during one of her visits to the hotel, and in 1979 (one imagines much to the owner's delight) a rusty iron key – later found to be the key to the box that held her diary – was discovered in her room. Atatürk, the founder of the Turkish Republic, also stayed in the hotel on several occasions. His preferred room (which was, rather ominously, room 101), is now preserved as a museum and includes many of his personal belongings.

The hotel contains 145 rooms and six suites over its six floors, and several restaurants, including the main restaurant, Pasha café at street level, a patisserie, and the Mirror Restaurant on the terrace overlooking the Golden Horn. Also in the hotel, as famous as Pera Palas itself, is the unchanged Orient Bar (p. 157), once the haunt of spies. For those who are after history with a little mystery, Pera Palas is the right address.

eat

With the immigration of peoples from Asia and Europe to Anatolia over the centuries, it is not surprising that the food of Turkey has become one of the world's great cuisines. Whipping up meals for generations of emperors and sultans, imperial chefs were able to create suitably grand and complex dishes using ingredients from every corner of the empire. Istanbul's modern restaurant culture has continued to absorb culinary influences from around the globe, and many fine international restaurants have sprung up all over the city. However, true Istanbulians head for corner meyhanes, the bustling neighbourhood cafés that serve the fish-of-the-day with a glass of rakı.

92 **Kıyı**

29 Kefeliköy Caddesi 126

The concentration of fish restaurants per square metre in Tarabya, a district once the summer resort of the aristocracy, is nothing short of staggering. Kıyı, which opened in the 1960s, is probably the most famous – and celebrity-studded – of them all, not only in Tarabya, but throughout the city. 'Same address, same patronage,' maintains co-owner Yorgi Sabuncu, when asked about the key to Kıyı's success. 'We are constantly renewing ourselves while doing our best to keep the same old spirit.' This warm and welcoming vibe is perpetuated by the friendly staff and peaceful décor. The walls are covered with timber panelling and a large collection of photographs and paintings by Turkish artists such as Ara Güler and Bedri Baykam. Together with seasonal fish and *meze*, the menu also includes such traditional favourites as *barbunya pilaki* (a cold dish made with dried kidney beans and olive oil) and *arnavut ciğeri* (fried liver). For dinner, reservations are a must at Kıyı.

IMPERIAL AUTHENTICITY

30 **Asitane Restaurant**

41 Kariye Camii Sokak 18

Unusually, Kariye Hotel, next to the Kariye Müzesi (Chora Museum), is more famous for its sophisticated eatery Asitane than for its rooms. Consequently, the clientele consists primarily of local residents instead of tourists. The large and airy Asitane Restaurant serves imperial Ottoman cuisine, incorporating Central Asian, Anatolian, Middle Eastern and Balkan flavours, resulting from the intensive research undertaken at three palace kitchens (Dolmabahçe, Topkapı and Edirne) to test and recreate long-forgotten imperial dishes, whose recipes were traditionally kept secret. Some of the rediscovered dishes on the menu, such as veal in apple sauce, were served at the circumcision feast held for two of Süleyman's sons in 1539. The location might be off the beaten track, but Asitane is the one and only restaurant in the city where intrepid diners can experience such unlikely-sounding treats as almond soup. This is a restaurant for the serious culinary adventurer.

14 Lokanta

16 Meşrutiyet Caddesi 149/1

Mehmet Gürs is the name behind Lokanta, the restaurant that put Istanbul on the global culinary map. One of the city's busiest chefs, during the last few years he has produced three eateries, a catering company, two cookbooks and two TV programmes. In his signature restaurant, housed on the ground floor of the city's prominent nightlife complex NuPera (p. 160), Gürs, a native of Finland, serves modern Mediterranean- and Scandinavian-influenced dishes, emphasizing fresh and simple organic ingredients. The pizzas are fantastic, but the menu is full of must-try dishes. The small annex just across the main restaurant is dedicated to its acclaimed *ufak yemekler* (small tasting dishes). If you are after a good wine, the list offers some of Turkey's best, along with international vintages. With its high ceiling, rough brick walls, well-spaced tables and large bar, Lokanta guarantees quality cooking in a friendly and relaxed atmosphere. Upstairs on the terrace is rooftop bar NuTeras, where cocktails are accompanied by the breathtaking view.

THE FISHER KING

30 Balıkçı Sabahattin

6 Seyit Hasan Kuyu Sokak 50

Of the hundreds of fish restaurants in Istanbul, one of the best, Balıkçı Sabahattin, is located not on the sea, but in a three-storey wooden house in the Cankurtaran region of historic Sultanahmet. This restaurant differs from its competitors not only in its location, but also in its menu, which bans any kind of farmed fish. Owner Sabahattin Korkmaz has even teamed up with three divers, who keep the restaurant supplied with the season's best. This passion for freshness doesn't stop with fish, as Aegean herbs and olive oil from the Mudanya region are shipped in daily. Korkmaz began working in his father's restaurant when he was ten years old, and his long experience is evident in the *lakerda* (salted tuna) and *çiroz* (dried mackerel). Reservations are essential, but it is worth the extra planning: dining al fresco in the summer months in the garden, or at one of the streetside tables underneath fishing nets and coloured bulbs, is an unforgettable experience.

14 **Changa**

Housed in a beautiful 1903 Art Nouveau building, Changa is the premier fusion restaurant of Istanbul. Owners Savaş Ertunç and Tarık Beyazıt turned their backs on careers as CEOs and started up Changa (meaning 'mix' in Swahili) in 2000, in the then less than salubrious Sıraselviler district. After bringing in well-known New Zealander Peter Gordon as consultant chef, Changa quickly became a firm Istanbul favourite. Serving Asian-Mediterranean fusion dishes, it was the only Turkish restaurant among *Restaurant Magazine*'s top fifty restaurants in the world. As part of its semi-industrial décor, a glass window set into the floor enables diners to watch the action in the basement kitchen (fortunately, the window is one-way), and the sleek bar at the entrance serves drinks in shot glasses made entirely of ice. In 2001, Changa and Peter Gordon opened a sister restaurant, The Providores, in London's Marylebone High Street.

80 **Ulus 29 + Club 29**

18 Ahmet Adnan Saygun Caddesi

Zeynep Fadıllıoğlu's unique approach to interiors is instantly recognizable in this lavishly decorated restaurant. Having designed London restaurant Chintamani, her interpretation of ethnic themes has already gone global. She is not only the architect behind Ulus 29's interior, but also owns the restaurant together with husband Metin Fadıllıoğlu. With its hilltop location within Ulus Parkı (p. 88), and views of the Bosphorus through floor-to-ceiling windows, Ulus 29's setting couldn't be more breathtaking. The food is a mixture of French, Italian and Turkish cuisines, reflecting the nationalities of the chefs in the kitchen. Among the classic dishes on offer are kebap with yoghurt and grilled sea bass, and the ever-popular *fındık lahmacun* (mini meat pizzas). Recently, Ulus 29 has added sushi and sashimi. If you have not yet tired of the Ulus experience after your meal, you can dance the night away at next-door Club 29, where, with its velvet-upholstered daybeds and multitude of cushions, the Arabian Nights fantasy continues until dawn.

66 | Park Şamdan
12 Mim Kemal Öke Caddesi 18

One restaurant that is a permanent fixture in the hearts of Istanbul's diners is Park Şamdan. Since 1981, long before the stampede of chic boutiques and trendy bistros arrived in Nişantaşı, Park Şamdan has been serving traditional fare in the neighbourhood. The interior is refined modern luxury without the frills, with leather banquettes, white linen tablecloths and mirrored walls, and a Chesterfield sofa, lounge chairs and coffee tables providing a comfortable seating area at the rear of the restaurant. Park Şamdan is a popular spot for the ultimate power-lunch, catering to suited and booted businessmen puffing expensive cigars within its gentlemen's club interior. The menu is primarily Turkish, occasionally even offering *kokoreç* (fried sheep intestines) as a daily special. The porch opening onto the park next door is more casual in its décor, and is a favourite haunt of Nişantaşı's ladies who lunch. Reservations are a must for dinner.

HOT SPOT IN THE CITY
92 | Feriye Lokantası
5 Çırağan Caddesi 124

Today part of the Kabataş Cultural Complex (also housing a cinema and exhibition hall), Feriye Lokantası, an Ottoman restaurant offering seasonal menus and organic ingredients, is housed in a 19th-century building near the glamorous Çırağan Palace Hotel. Behind this elegant venue is celebrity chef Vedat Başaran, who has also served as head chef for a recent NATO conference while turning out authentic Ottoman recipes. Summer is the best time of the year to enjoy Feriye's charms. Every beachside restaurant worth its sea salt boasts of the stunning views, but those waiting to be savoured at Feriye Lokantası when the tables are brought out onto the promenade terrace are truly something else. After sating your appetite, natural honey and olive oil are also available at the restaurant for purchase.

106 Café Zanzibar

2 Cemil Topuzlu Caddesi 112

Despite its casual name, Café Zanzibar is in fact an elegantly chic restaurant that serves an equally chic (and rich) menu. When it first opened in Nişantaşı, Café Zanzibar was a mid-sized bistro with a safari décor. The owners soon acquired the adjacent store, and began to operate as fully-fledged restaurant. The name remained, but the animal-print cushions were swept away and replaced with dark furniture and moody lighting. Soon another branch opened on the Asian side of the city. Now housed in a 19th-century mansion designed by August Jachmund (who also designed the Sirkeci train station, see p. 38), Café Zanzibar's interior is dominated by the sheer glamour of the original setting, with neoclassical trimmings on the walls and ceiling, and large oval mirrors bringing the sea view inside. As for the menu, diners clamour for the tender grilled beef medallions with herbs, smoked salmon paté, and Café Zanzibar's justly famous *tarte tatin* (upside-down apple tart). They make the best in town.

30 Darüzziyafe

37 Şifahane Sokak 6

Located in the former kitchens of the Süleymaniye Camii is Darüzziyafe, one of Istanbul's more frequently overlooked restaurants. Today it is comprised of two side-by-side rooms, the Kanuni room (dominated by Süleyman's imperial monogram) and the Sinan room (named after the city's most revered architect), surrounded by a beautiful garden. The old wash basin and copper plates are leftovers from the kitchens' previous life, as is the enormous plane tree outside. During the summer months, diners can enjoy a meal under its leafy shadow. Darüzziyafe's menu offers a variety of Turkish and Ottoman dishes, including Süleymaniye soup (made from winter vegetables and lentils) and *Yufkalı Darüzziyafe Köftesi* (meatballs flavoured with ten different spices, pistachio and mushroom, wrapped in phyllo dough). For afters try *Fukara Keşkülü*, a milky dessert sent on Fridays past by the Ottoman sultans to the poor. Although it is a commonly prepared dessert, only Darüzziyafe is true to the traditional recipe and includes pistachio.

92 La Maison

3 Müvezzi Caddesi 63

Situated on the Çırağan ridge, La Maison is one of the best (if not the best) French restaurants in Istanbul. This rooftop restaurant, housed within the thirty-four-room La Maison Hotel (itself considered to be the city's first-ever boutique hotel) offers a sophisticated (and pricey) dining experience within its serene and cosy interior. With a French and Turkish team in the kitchen, La Maison serves up such aristocratic dishes as crab crêpe in mushroom and cream sauce, quail in prune sauce, and roast duck with orange and cognac, which are finished off with a soufflé and always accompanied by a good selection of French wines. The restaurant can seat sixty, and can accommodate up to eighty during the summer months when it makes use of the lovely terrace with its magnificent views of the Bosphorus. As a testament to La Maison's achievements, Le Cordon Bleu, the world-famous culinary arts school, has selected the restaurant to host its food and drink festival in Turkey.

 Paper Moon

12 Ahmet Adnan Saygun Caddesi

Considered to be the most elegant and most expensive restaurant in the city, Paper Moon is truly something to experience. The restaurant, located within the Akmerkez shopping mall, has been catering to an upscale clientele since it opened in 1995, and has become the venue of choice for high-powered business meetings. Guests are welcomed into an L-shaped bar, which leads into separate dining rooms with comfy chairs and snow-white tablecloths. The soothing interior, created by designer

Tony Chi, was found worthy of the Restaurant and Institutions design award in 1997. Every two years a new chef arrives from Italy, but the rest of the staff at Paper Moon, like the clientele, hardly changes. Diners come for the delicious Sicilian-style crispy pizzas and *taglioni neri con salmone,* and, from the antipasti menu, the mouth-watering *carpaccio di polipo.* Finishing one's meal with an espresso and a *limoncello* is a must, as is making a reservation in advance.

106 Kanaat Lokantası
18 Selmani Pak Caddesi 25

Since 1933, Kanaat Lokantası, which has an approximate turnover of 1,200 people a day, has been serving traditional Ottoman and Turkish cuisine at its Üsküdar location. Though menus are scattered on the tables, at Kanaat no one bothers to look at them. Daily specials are displayed in a long glass case, from which diners make their choice. *Elbasan tava* (lamb) and *patlıcan kebabı* (aubergine kebap) are favourites, but these are just two of the over 100 dishes on offer every day. The story of Kanaat is the story of Vahdettin Kargılı, a native of Albania who spent his early days selling ice cream from a cart. Today the second generation of the Kargılı family runs Kanaat, but Vahdettin's original ice cream is still very much in demand.

SOUFFLÉ GOOD
66 Mimkemal 19
11 Mim Kemal Öke Caddesi 19

Istanbul's foodies became acquainted with the creative cooking style of Şemsa Denizsel through her lunchtime venue, Kantin (p. 75). Now the recently-opened Mimkemal 19, set up in partnership with Sinan Aşkın, has become the new favourite. The location is below ground level, but Mimkemal 19 gets plenty of daylight from the floor-to-ceiling windows opening onto the patio garden at the rear. The interior adopts a less-is-more approach, creating a monochrome elegance with its chocolate-brown leather banquettes and dark wooden tables, complemented by ornate light fixtures. The long bar is ideal for pre-dinner cocktails. When it is time to choose from the menu, don't miss the bluefish tartare if it's in season. Otherwise try the cheese soufflé served with bacon and spring onion, or the duck schnitzel. The wine list includes both local and international vintages.

66 Boğaziçi Borsa Restaurant

5 Lütfi Kırdar Kongre Sarayı

It all started in 1927 with a small à la carte restaurant in Bahçekapı, which subsequently expanded into a family-run chain serving traditional Turkish dishes. Such was the popularity of the restaurants that they were more than a match for the onslaught of American fast-food chains opening throughout the city. The latest incarnation, Boğaziçi Borsa, opened in 1996 and retained the traditional focus on home-grown fare. Located along with its sister restaurant, Loft (p. 68), within the rather less than aesthetically pleasing Lütfi Kırdar Kongre Sarayı (Istanbul Convention & Exhibition Centre), the restaurant's modern décor, generous seating capacity (it can seat over 500 diners) and excellent service, along with a seriously good wine list, make Boğaziçi Borsa the venue of choice for Istanbul's smart set. The dessert *hurmalı incir tatlısı* (made with figs and dates) is a highlight of the menu, so make sure to leave space for a full portion.

66 The House Café

20 Atiye Sokak 10/1

Its enduring success has spawned many imitators, none of whom have managed to surpass The House Café. From the day it opened in 2002, local residents have adopted it as a second home, clustering around the large common table that dominates the main room. The café, thanks to its friendly staff and its owners, Ramazan Üren and Canan Baltacıoğlu, is busy all day long. The surprisingly tiny kitchen delivers superlative comfort food (and bakes its own bread), while the small bar just across the entrance serves the best coffee in town. Take your pick from specials on the blackboard or go with the ever-popular House Burger. Regulars are brought their favourite choices immediately without being asked. The mismatched furniture (bargain finds mixed in with custom-made designs) creates a dynamic atmosphere. And if you take a sudden fancy to the chair you are sitting on, you can take it home with you at a very reasonable price. A beautifully decorated and magically illuminated garden at the rear end of the café provides al fresco dining in the summer.

14 **Hacı Abdullah**
8 Sakızağacı Caddesi 17

Hacı Abdullah, the oldest restaurant in Istanbul (or so it claims), received a facelift in 2000, at the expense, some would argue, of its historic character. Fortunately, the slick and shiny interior has not altered the menu, and the food is as good as ever. Since 1888 Hacı Abdullah, the first restaurant to be endorsed by an Ottoman Sultan (Abdülhamid II, to be precise), has been serving up a variety of Ottoman and Turkish flavours. The menu is vast, so first-timers are advised to try the Special Hacı Abdullah Plate, which includes four separate hot dishes. Hacı Abdullah is the ultimate culinary destination for foodies wishing to satisfy their curiosity about authentic Turkish cuisine. The stained glass dome just above the mezzanine floor is also worthy of admiration.

30 **Pandeli**

18 Mısır Çarşısı 1

At the main entrance of Mısır Çarşısı, guests venturing down the steep steps to the left will find themselves at Pandeli, one of the oldest restaurants in Istanbul. Named after its founder, Pandeli Çobanoğlu, in 1901, the aqua-tiled restaurant with its beautiful domes is architecturally stunning. Today run by Pandeli's son, Hristo Çobanoğlu, together with Cemal Biberci, Pandeli continues to function as the original owner intended. 'He always considered his customers as his guests,' recalls Biberci, adding that

Pandeli often refused to take their money. If Pandeli is not entertaining the likes of Mikhail Gorbachev or Juan Carlos II of Spain, you may be lucky enough to find a vacant table by the small windows overlooking the Golden Horn. Highlights of the extensive menu are sea bass in paper, leg of lamb with vegetables, and aubergine pie. Guests who still have some room left should try the Pandeli Sweet, a medley of several famous Turkish desserts. Unfortunately, Pandeli is open only for lunch.

drink

The diversity that dominates and energizes this city is reflected in the drinking habits of its residents. The choices — and drinks — are endless, from the ubiquitous traditional tipple rakı, served at local meyhanes and also called 'lion's milk' because of its colour and alcoholic punch, to the cosmopolitan cocktails available in Istanbul's rapidly multiplying bars at the other end of the trendy scale. When the need for caffeine is pressing, do as the locals do and visit an old-fashioned coffee house to sip bitter Turkish coffee from a tulip-shaped glass.

14 Leb-i Derya
19 Kumbaracı Yokuşu 115

Istanbul is full of surprises, and visitors often come across the most panoramic views in unexpected places. Walk down the Kumbaracı Yokuşu, a steep road full of old apartment buildings, and enter number 115. The lift will take you to the sixth floor, and a staircase leads you to the seventh and your destination, the delightful restaurant Leb-i Derya. If you can tear your eyes from the staggering view visible through the large windows, take a seat at the bar or at one of the wooden tables. The menu offers dazzling array of cocktails, including *Yasak Elma* (Forbidden Apple), a mixture of Martini Bianco, Absolut, Cointreau, lemon and apple juice, and *Masal* (Fairy Tale), which, although no longer appearing on the menu, is still a best-seller. Also offering a full menu of contemporary dishes (try *kıtırlı biftek,* slices of beef in tomato sauce served with spicy croutons), Leb-i Derya is a place to return to again and again.

30 Pierre Loti Café
44 Gümüşsuyu Balmumcu Sokak 1

Pierre Loti was a French romantic novelist who chose Turkey as his second home. After stumbling upon this traditional coffee-house on the outskirts of Eyüp in the late 19th century, Loti became a frequent visitor, and the café has been known by his name ever since. Today visited by artists in search of inspiration and lovers already inspired by the romantic view over the Golden Horn, the Pierre Loti Café is a modest establishment offering nothing more than Turkish coffee warmed over charcoal, tea served in tulip-shaped glasses, a spot of *nargile*, and a few snacks. The interior is decorated in the traditional coffee-house style, with couches, copper tables and low wooden stools. The small glass cabinet next to the entrance displays original editions of Loti's books, and the tiny kitchen is covered with İznik tiles glistening with steam from the boiling coffee and tea pots. Recently, with the addition of a souvenir shop, Pierre Loti has become a little touristy, but still there is no better setting in which to taste authentic (if bitter) Turkish coffee.

OLD-FASHIONED PATISSERIE

106 **Baylan Pastanesi**

13 Muvakkithane Caddesi 19

Baylan is so famous for its *cup griye* (ice cream with caramel sauce, toasted almonds, vanilla, pistachios, crème Chantilly and cat's tongue biscuits) that dedicated fans cross continents (or at least the Bosphorus) to get their fix. First established in 1923 in a quiet Beyoğlu street under the name L'Orient, owner Philip Lenas changed it to Baylan in 1934 in accordance with the new law that insisted on the conversion of foreign names into Turkish ones. In due course, the present branch opened up on the Asian shore, and subsequently left its predecessor far behind in the popularity stakes. Baylan's owner Harry Lenas (Philip's elder son) received his patisserie training in Vienna. The *cup griye* is still prepared and served in the traditional manner, in an old-fashioned décor of formica tables. Some newcomers, such as pear pie, have also made an appearance on the menu.

BOSPHORUS CLASSIC

92 **Bebek Bar**

18 Cevdet Paşa Caddesi 34

Bebek Bar, occupying the ground level of Bebek Hotel, is beloved of Istanbul's natives and is consistently chosen year after year as the best bar in town. With its perfect seaside location, this landmark bar is an ideal place for a few aprés-work cocktails while watching the sun set over the Bosphorus. Inside are dark wooden tables and leather-upholstered chairs, and the walls are hung with caricatures of famous barflies and fake diplomas on alcoholic studies. Rattan chairs line the veranda, a restful and romantic spot to start the day with a pot of coffee or to end it with a glass of wine. Bar snacks are available throughout the day. Faultless service, excellent stock (especially of wine) and unbeatable views make Bebek Bar a top choice for local drinkers.

92 **Pando**

2 Mumcu Sokak 5

Ask any Istanbulian where the best breakfast in town is, and you will soon be directed to Pando, a tiny eatery-cum-shop. Containing only four tables (the number increases to five during the summer months with the addition of an outside table) and situated just a few steps away from the Beşiktaş fish market, Pando is famous for its vivid blue framework, its grumpy owner and his dislike of large banknotes, and, most importantly, its delicious milk cream. Though Pando has been written up many times by the world's press, its owner steadfastly refuses to give his shop a facelift. Breakfasts here include a plate filled with natural honey, milk cream, Gemlik olives and white cheese – the truly Turkish way to start the day.

BOZA FOR SALE!

30 **Vefa Bozacısı**

23 Katip Çelebi Caddesi 104/1

Boza, a thick fermented millet drink revered for its nourishing properties, is the oldest known Turkish beverage, best enjoyed on chilly winter nights. Traditionally *boza* was purchased from street-vendors, who carried their wares in large metal jugs through the city. Today these mobile *boza*-sellers are a rarity, but Vefa Bozacısı, founded by Hacı Salih Bey in 1876, still operates in its nostalgic premises. The well-preserved shop, now synonymous with the drink, is today run by Bey's great-great-grandsons, who have added balsamic vinegar and pomegranate juice to the répertoire. *Boza* is still a favourite drink among the locals, and is popular with adventurous tourists. Though widely available in bottles at supermarkets, the ritual of drinking *boza* freshly poured into a glass from a large jug at Vefa is a true Istanbul experience.

SPIES LIKE US

14 Orient Bar

23 Pera Palas Hotel Meşrutiyet Caddesi 98–100

You don't have to be a guest at the hotel to enjoy the nostalgic and mysterious atmosphere of Pera Palas (p. 136). The legendary Orient Bar, located in the lobby of the hotel, whisks diners back to a time of intrigue and elegance. The turn-of-the-century interior is lavishly decorated, and includes a huge oriental carpet, topped with comfy velvet-upholstered chairs. Once frequented by local intellectuals, as well as more infamous characters (Mata Hari and Kim Philby have both raised a glass or two here), the tea room has become a magnet for tourists eager to absorb any atmosphere the spies might have left behind. Despite the sky-high prices, the romantic mood and intriguing history make Orient Bar a must.

OUT OF THE TIME CAPSULE

14 Patisserie Markiz

18 İstiklal Caddesi 360

After an absence of twenty-three years, Patisserie Markiz re-opened its doors in the Passage Orientale in Beyoğlu (then called Pera) in 2003. Opened in 1940 and named after the Parisian chocolates Marquise de Sevigne, Markiz was popular with Pera's smart set until the premises were sold to an auto parts dealer in 1980. A journalist and former patron, Haldun Taner, bemoaned its fate in the national press, and the Higher Council of Monuments stepped in to save the patisserie. Today, Patisserie Markiz – originally designed by Alexandre Vallaury, the architect of Pera Palas (p. 136) – is back to its former Art Nouveau glory, complete with faience panels designed by J. A. Arnoux. The mid-19th-century arcade in which it is housed is somewhat less sympathetically restored. Favourite bakery treats from Markiz include chestnut cake, baklava and macara.

30 **Safa Meyhanesi**
1 İmrahor İlyas Bey Caddesi 169

The origins of Safa Meyhanesi, an authentic and distinguished *meyhane* in the historic district of Yedikule, are uncertain, but according to owner Arif Kızıltay, who belongs to the second generation of the family to run the café since 1948, it is more than 110 years old. 'We never thought of moving to a central location because we would never catch the same atmosphere,' he explains. The high ceiling, off-white walls hung with old Turkish portraits, and glass wall-cabinets containing *rakı* bottles certainly ooze nostalgia. The only vaguely modern item within the interior is the chandelier which dominates the room, and its predecessor was only replaced because the cleaning boy dropped it. As for the food, Safa, in true *meyhane* style, serves twenty varieties of cold *meze*. Safa Meyhanesi's fried liver is famous, but in a setting as lush as this, everything is wonderful.

66 **Armani Caffe**
15 Maçka Caddesi 35

COSMOPOLITAN COCKTAILS

Milanese architect Giulio Mongeri designed many of Istanbul's most recognizable buildings during the first quarter of the 20th century. Among them are the church of St Antoine and Maçka Palas, two of the city's particular architectural gems. Built in 1922 and once the home of writer and poet Abdülhak Hamid Tarhan, Maçka Palas was bought by the Doğuş Holding Company a few years ago and after careful restoration, now houses the Emporio Armani and Gucci stores, as well as one of world's largest Armani Caffes. Istanbul's version serves Italian fare in its beautiful garden terrace, but the real action starts in the evenings when the city's office workers drop by for a few drinks at the bar. The cocktails, prepared according to the special recipes of chef Antonio C. Lombardi, are the most

14 **Yakup 2**

21 Asmalı Mescit Sokak 35–37

It isn't the food or the décor that makes Yakup 2 special, but rather the owner Yakup Arslan himself that attracts the crowd to this *meyhane* every night of the week. (His method of getting customers to leave their tables at closing time is particularly memorable.) Nearby *meyhane* Refik (p. 23) is run by Arslan's uncle, who brought his nephew from Rize to to the Asmalımescit area to work as his apprentice. After years of careful training, Arslan took over his uncle's business in 1974. Eight years later, when the popularity of his restaurant outgrew its original premises, Arslan moved the newly renamed Yakup 2 to its present location. Yakup 2's popularity with its regulars is legendary. During his stay in Istanbul, German musician Detlef Glanert composed a concerto in its honour, and several aspiring poets, after enough glasses of *rakı*, write devotional odes on their napkins.

92 **Vogue**

1 Süleyman Seba Caddesi

Vogue, located in the penthouse suite of a thirteen-storey building and possessing stunning views over the Bosphorus, is undeniably the city's most popular restaurant-cum-bar. Vogue is best enjoyed in the summer, when the weather is warm and the cocktails are at their most refreshing when served on the surrounding terrace. But whatever the season, Vogue is always thronging with jet-setters, thanks to its global cuisine and cocktail bar, which offers a vast menu divided into classics, frozen favourites and the exotic. Vogue's famed wine list carries around 200 international vintages, as well as domestic varieties. Sipping a Mojito on the terrace at sunset, with music provided by DJs in the background, sets the scene for a perfect evening in Istanbul.

CAFÉ IN THE MUSEUM

14 **İstanbul Modern Café**
42 Meclis-i Mebusan Caddesi Antrepo 4

With excellent views of the sea and the peninsula, the café at İstanbul Modern seems to attract more visitors than the museum itself. This shouldn't come as too much of a surprise, as it is managed by the Borsa Group, who also own Loft (p. 68) and Boğaziçi Borsa (p. 149). The interior is dominated by the colour red and 20th-century modern furniture, including Eames chairs, creating a charmingly vivid atmosphere. The graphic pattern of the red wallpaper continues along the metalwork of the large rectangular bar at the centre, where diners can order coffee and a vast selection of cocktails, beer and wine. There is also a breakfast-to-lunch menu (scheduled to include dinner in the near future) serving salads, pasta and grilled meats.

SCENE TO BE SEEN

14 **NuPera + NuTeras**
15 Meşrutiyet Caddesi 149

Occupying a 200-year-old building, NuPera has brought new life to the area since its opening in 2001. Prior to NuPera's arrival, Istanbul's nightlife was based in Etiler, and it never entered the heads of party girls and boys to come to Beyoğlu to dance the night away. Today the clubs and bars are all clustered in Beyoğlu, and NuPera is simply the best of the lot. On the ground floor is the restaurant Lokanta (p. 141), and next to it is the lounge/bar area, heaving with a stylish crowd during the week and with everybody else at weekends. Manned by local and international DJs, the downstairs club is open four days a week. The rooftop NuTeras is only open during the summer months, but is well worth a return visit for the mesmerizing views of the Golden Horn.

Viktor Levi

9 Hamalbaşı Caddesi 12

Despite its venerable status as one of Istanbul's oldest wine bars (there is also nearby Pano, owned by the same management), because of changing owners and occasional manifestations as a coffee house, the original décor of Viktor Levi has long since vanished. Yet with the help of plenty of wrought iron, wooden tables and wall mosaics, recent owners have tried to recapture the atmosphere originally created in 1941 by Viktor Levi, a Jewish wine supplier and the name behind the present-day wine bar. Among the house wines, No. 59 and the eponymous Viktor Levi are perpetual favourites. White wines include Rebeka and Vasilaki, and Adakarası, Papazkarası and Daryo are among the reds.

DANCING ON THE CEILING

Buz Teşvikiye

21 Abdi İpekçi Caddesi 42/2

When it first opened on the second floor of an office building, Buz, with its stylish décor and superb cocktails, instantly became a hot spot for Istanbul's night-time revellers. Despite the assured fabulousness of the cocktails, their prices are a bit steep, as are those of the menu offerings. But Istanbul's bohos are always willing to embrace the eccentric, and Buz Teşvikiye provides eccentricity in spades. After moving to new premises in 2002, owners Lal Dedeoğlu and Ender Sanal decided to bring some of the old interior with them. The result is a new look on the ground, including Polaroids of regulars crowding the walls, and the old look adorning the ceiling. So, while sipping your Buz Martini (with thyme and cubed lemon) or frozen tangerine Tequila, if you notice a table or chair hanging upside-down above your head, it doesn't mean that you've had a few too many. It's all just part of the crazy décor at Buz Teşvikiye.

14 Sefahathane

3 Atlas Pasajı Girişi

Located in Atlas Pasajı just off the busy İstiklal Caddesi, Sefahathane has been serving drinks in its narrow, corridor-like space for the last fifteen years, and has become a fixture on the Beyoğlu nightlife circuit. Some of its devoted regulars are pre-club visitors, but many do not leave Sefahathane's cosy interior until the small hours, sipping drinks at the long bar. Cocktails on offer include *caiproska* (vodka, lemon juice and sugar), drinks made from frozen pear, and hot wine, but the tipple of choice at Sefahathane is beer. This is one of the rare places in Beyoğlu where revellers can find good (if deafening) music accompanied by quality service.

VIEWS FROM ABOVE
14 360 İstanbul
10 İstiklal Caddesi 311/32

Probably the most hotly-anticipated new venue of the
last few years, 360 İstanbul's stunning location and
celebrity owners ensured that it made the headlines even
before it opened. Occupying a rooftop location atop the
historic and popular Mısır Apartmanı, 360 İstanbul appears
as a glass box perched on top of the building, and offers
mesmerizing 360-degree views of the sea and the city.
Mısır Apartmanı is adjacent to the beautiful church of St
Antoine, and its bell tower serves as a perfect backdrop to
the restaurant. The ultra-modern interior is black and
white, with two enormous circular sofas (one red and one
green) designed by Derin (p. 70) to break the monotony.
The large bar at the centre offers endless varieties of
cocktails, including house cocktail 360 (Smirnoff Citrus,
Archers, passion fruit and apple juice) and Beyoğlu Orgasm
(Baileys, Amaretto and Kahlua). For the adventurous, Eau
de Haliç is a dangerous mixture of *rakı* and melon liqueur.

shop

When it comes to parting with one's cash, the Grand Bazaar, with its vast selection of carpets, clothing, jewelry and handicrafts, is the place to start. But for those with less stamina and bargaining know-how, the city offers everything from designer labels to quirky, individual pieces. Turkey has produced several high-profile couture designers in recent years, including Hussein Chalayan and Ümit Ünal, and they, along with smaller local designers, have ensured that fashion's fickle eye is focused firmly on Istanbul. As expected with a city that has produced such beautiful crafts as İznik tiles and hand-woven kilims, Istanbul's housewares are particularly covetable.

52 **A La Turca**

19 Faikpaşa Yokuşu 4

With its lack of signboard outside the premises, visitors often miss A La Turca, a real treasure trove of Ottoman and Anatolian antiques. Opening in 1998 in the neighbourhood of Çukurcuma, owner Erkal Aksoy converted the four-storey house into a showroom to trade antique carpets and *kilims*, as well as paintings, ceramics, manuscripts and other decorative objects. Aksoy was one of the pioneers of the changing face of Çukurcuma, and it is thanks to him that the once-derelict street is now home to the city's best art galleries and design shops. Browsing among A La Turca's treasures can feel like visiting the private home of a serious collector, rather than a shop. Aksoy considers anyone who passes through the door of his magnificent showroom as an honoured guest, and welcomes shoppers with home-made cherry liqueur and butter cookies. If you wish to be on the receiving end of Aksoy's hospitality, be sure to arrange an appointment before ringing the bell.

30 **Mısır Çarşısı**

17 Mısır Çarşısı

Compared to the infamous Grand Bazaar, Mısır Çarşısı (known as the spice bazaar, or the Egyptian bazaar) is rather small, and, thankfully, less touristy. Built in 1660 to provide funds for the upkeep of the adjacent mosque (Yeni Camii), this L-shaped bazaar was once totally occupied by spice shops. Although over time some of the shops have turned their attentions to gifts and jewelry, most are still faithful to the original concept. The bazaar is chaotic, with stallholders yelling from all directions and urging shoppers, some more forcefully than others, to part with their cash. Be prepared for constant haggling, which often ends abruptly with an invitation into the shop for a cup of tea. Within the bazaar, tea is offered in around ten different languages. Whatever your culinary inspiration (or indeed, aspiration), there is a wide range of spices, from cinnamon to real saffron, all temptingly delicious and colourful in their sack containers. Beauty products such as olive oil soaps and henna are available as well. This bazaar is a truly sensory experience.

30 **L'Orient**

21 Şerif Ağa Sokak 22-23

Forty-two years ago, Murat Bilir used to come to the bazaar to earn his pocket money trading Anatolian metalwork. Today Bilir has become one of the most renowned figures in the area, frequently asked to give lectures on metalwork, and has written many newspaper and magazine articles on the subject. His tiny store (only five-and-a-half square metres) sells water pitchers, samovars, lanterns, covered dishes, ink and quill sets, and shadow puppets. Particularly popular among the latter are the figures of Karagöz and Hacivat, the main characters of the Turkish shadow-puppet tradition, created by Göksel Erdal, whose early puppets are now exhibited in the Louvre. Bilir's stock is impressive, but it is his vast knowledge and passion, and his willingness to share them, that attract visitors to this unique shop.

14 **Ümit Ünal**

31 Ensiz Sokak 3

A designer with an avant-garde edge, Ümit Ünal started designing fashion collections in the early 1990s and has subsequently won many awards, including the 1997 Fashion Festival International Designer award. His interpretations of different walks of life, such as the Himalaya (2001) and Fallen Angels (2004) collections, have gained him a sound reputation in the fashion industry. Housed in a 19th-century English building that also hosts the biannual Tünel Festival, his atelier-cum-showroom is worth a visit. Dominated by neutral colours, with old wooden doors collected from Aegean villages, it forms the perfect backdrop to his delicate creations. Ümit Ünal's recent collection, La Russie (2005), took its inspiration from the Russian Empire, and is described by its creator as 'the new romanticism, the new militarism and the new aristocracy.'

Until the 1970s, the concept of pret-a-porter was but a gleam in the Turkish consumer's eye. Then along came Osman Boyner, the youngest member of a family that has been in the textile business for over 200 years. Founded in 1971, his store Beymen (a combination of the Turkish and English words for 'men') quickly became the last word in men's ready-to-wear. Collections for women and children soon followed, and Beymen continued to be a retail pioneer for the last few decades, opening branches nationwide. The latest addition to the Beymen empire is a megastore in Nişantaşı. Occupying 3,500 square metres over seven floors, this is one of the few places where shoppers can treat themselves from head (at famous hairdresser Erdem Kıramer's salon) to toe. Located on the ground floor is the Beymen Brasserie, frequented by Istanbul's beautiful young things, stopping for an espresso before braving the army of paparazzi clustered outside. Other locations are in the Akmerkez mall (Etiler) and Bağdat Caddesi (Asian shore).

66 **Gönül Paksoy**

17 Atiye Sokak 1/3 and 6/A

The multi-talented Gönül Paksoy designs everything from clothes to jewelry to shoes, and even dolls made of fabric. In true modern multi-tasking style, she is also a renowned culinary artist. Her two boutiques, both located in Atiye Sokak, have been beloved of Istanbul visitors and natives alike for the past fifteen years. Possessing a PhD in the use of plants as a source of natural dyes, she boldly experiments with textures and colours of antique fabrics, creating exceptional (and mostly one-off) dresses, shawls and kaftans, as well as handbags. As a designer who is uninterested in current fashion trends, the look of her collections do not radically change from season to season, but remain classically beautiful and eminently desirable. Her jewelry creations, which derive inspiration from archaeological artefacts, are as unique as her fashion designs.

66 **Zeynep Erol**

19 Atiye Sokak 8/3

Jewelry designer Zeynep Erol claims to be inspired by her emotions, and her efforts in interpreting her feelings have resulted in a collection of earrings, necklaces, rings and bracelets that combine gold and silver with precious and semi-precious stones in geometrical forms. Such pieces, she declares, are the 'natural clothes of mankind.' After completing a two-year course on metal techniques at the Grand Bazaar, Erol, a former ballet dancer, set up her atelier-cum-gallery-cum-retail space in 1994. Since then, the minimal setting of her showroom has been frequented by a dedicated stream of customers, pausing to admire the items of jewelry showcased on large wooden blocks and in glass cases projecting from the chalk-white walls. Zeynep Erol's collections can also be viewed at Aaron Faber in New York and the Electrum Gallery in London.

66 Paşabahçe
23 Teşvikiye Caddesi 117

In addition to setting the standards for Turkey's hand-made glassware industry, Paşabahçe (also the name of the region in which the factory was founded) has acquired reputation for being one of the leading glass manufacturers in the world. Founded in 1935, during recent years the company's products have become coveted objects both domestically and internationally, and snapped up by such global brands as Conran and Costa Boda. A number of Paşabahçe lifestyle stores have opened nationwide, where shoppers can find contemporary housewares along with reinterpretations of Anatolian and Ottoman forms, brought to life using ancient glass-blowing techniques. Among these collections are replicas of the world-famous Beykoz glassware, and hand-crafted glass and china objets d'art decorated with archaeological motifs inspired by past civilizations.

KNOCK ON WOOD
52 Stoa
25 Hayriye Sokak 18/1

Self-educated designer Tardu Kuman studied philosophy and spent a few years in Greece honing his DIY skills before opening his shop in 2001. From the outside, Stoa looks deceptively small. Inside, however, is a cavernous space showcasing some of the best wooden furniture and home accessories that Euros can buy (at least in Istanbul). Kuman uses both local and tropical woods, combining them with leather and other natural textiles to create furniture with a masculine edge. The chandeliers cast from bits of recycled metal are particularly striking. Unfortunately, Tardu Kuman has long since passed on his knowledge about designing them to his younger assistant.

THE BRIDE WORE LEATHER

Derishow

Yeşilçimen Sokak 17

A shopping emporium known for its quality designs, excellent displays and customer service, Derishow is a must for all dedicated followers of contemporary fashion. Originally trained as architects, husband-and-wife team Fatoş and Sancar Ahunbay founded Derishow in 1984 to trade their own line of clothing. The duo first started working solely with leather (*deri* means leather in Turkish), and soon added other materials to the range. Derishow subsequently became the first-ever internationally-renowned textile brand to come out of Turkey. In 1998, the home collection Mimarca, following the same contemporary and exclusive approach, was launched. Today the store, covering four floors, also offers limited-edition bridal wear designs. A coffee-bar on the ground floor provides welcome respite for weary shoppers and brides-to-be.

Housed in an Art Deco building in the heart of Çukurcuma, Accenturc is a design gallery-cum-shop spread over two floors. Owner Emine Turan studied jewelry design at the Gemological Institute of America in Los Angeles, and, upon returning to Istanbul, worked as a design manager at Turkish jewelry house Gilan (p. 87). A few years ago, recognizing the changing fortunes of Çukurcuma, Turan decided to set up shop there and opened Accenturc to display both her own elegant designs and the creations of other designers and artists. Primarily focusing on jewelry, Accenturc also carries a selection of furniture, lighting and textile designs, and sculptures by local artists. One section of the store is dedicated to changing exhibitions of paintings. Taking nature as her inspiration, Turan combines precious stones with semi-precious ones, along with leather, copper, crystal and ebony. She is a warm and welcoming hostess, and visiting her unique boutique is always a pleasure.

SEXUAL HEELING
66 **Erol Kundura**
24 Rumeli Caddesi 21-23

'I first fell in love with shoes, then with my wife,' boasts Erol Odabaşıoğlu. For a man who has been sketching shoes since he was eleven years old, being regarded as Turkey's most famous cobbler was a natural outcome. Odabaşıoğlu has been busy designing glamorous and sexy footwear since 1946, and has inevitably become known as Turkey's answer to Manolo Blahník (despite having been in the business long before Blahník became the high priest of footwear). At the beginning of his career, each shoe was crafted by hand, but today the company owns a factory equipped with the latest technology in shoe production. However, if patrons ask for a custom-made design, Odabaşıoğlu prefers to use traditional methods. Such an elegantly well-heeled shoe store as Erol Kundura is sure to have its famous regulars. Name any Turkish film star or singer, and Odabaşıoğlu will proudly tell you her shoe size.

The history of İznik tiles dates back to the 16th century. Reaching the height of their popularity at the end of 17th century, knowledge of production techniques all but vanished in the following centuries. After many years of research and experimentation, the İznik Foundation opened in 1993 in an attempt to reintroduce the 400-year-old art. The production of historically faithful İznik tiles requires careful craftsmanship, and the İznik Foundation uses the original techniques to create them. Its efforts can be seen in many of the mosques that dot the city. Because the tiles contain a network of pores that absorb sound waves, they create a pleasing acoustic effect. If you would like to take a piece of İznik tile back home with you, drop by the İznik Foundation's showroom. On display are vases, urns, bowls and, of course, tiles.

retreat

As do natives of all great cities, Istanbulians have their favourite weekend getaways, and take full advantage of the city's glorious surroundings. Despite the lack of of a city-wide underground system, buses will carry you (albeit slowly) up to the forests on the European side, and ferries will whisk you somewhat more efficiently to the islands and destinations across the Bosphorus. From the pristine beaches of the European side's Kilyos to the village atmosphere of Polonezköy on the Asian shore, bike-riding on the Princes' Islands to a little nature appreciation in Ağva, the beauty of greater Istanbul is at your service.

ISLAND HOPPING

The Princes' Islands: Beach, Beers and Buggies

- Büyükada
- Heybeliada
- Kınalıada
- Burgazadası

As if Cinderella's fairy godmother has waved her magic wand, within just 20 minutes you can be lazing on the beaches of the nine Princes' Islands, a world away from the chaos of the big city. The islands (*ada*), of which four (Büyükada, Heybeli, Kınalı and Burgaz) are inhabited, occupy the southeastern part of the Sea of Marmara, and during the days of the Byzantine Empire were used as places of exile because of their remoteness. With the ensuing improvements in sea travel, the islands were soon turned into serene and beautiful playgrounds by wealthy Istanbulians, quick to spot the ideal location for lavish summer residences.

Each island has its own unique personality, but a universal characteristic is the absence of cars. Horse-and-buggy tours are available, and bicycles can be rented at various points all over the islands. Büyükada, the former home of Leon Trotsky, is the largest (*büyük* means 'big') and most popular island. Visitors can eat seafood at Milto next to the pier, have a few beers and chips on one of the barrel tables in the main square, and visit the Aya Yorgi (St George's) monastery on the highest peak of the island, before retiring to the Splendid Palas Hotel.

Heybeli is almost entirely devoted to the Turkish Naval Academy, which occupies the site of a former Byzantine monastery and boasts the tomb of Sir Edward Barton, Elizabeth I's ambassador to Constantinople, within its grounds. The 19th-century Halki Palace Hotel, one of the oldest hotels in the area, is also on Heybeli, as is the Haghia Triada monastery, the Greek Orthodox school of theology controversially closed in the 1970s.

Kınalı, the nearest island to the city, is home to a large Armenian community, along with the modern Kınalıada Camii and the Armenian church, Surp Krikor Lusavoria. Burgaz, predominantly Greek and the smallest island of the group, is so tiny that visitors can walk the entire perimeter in two to three hours, stopping to visit the museum devoted to Turkish short-story writer, Sait Faik.

TWO RIVERS RUN THROUGH IT
Ağva: Rural Retreat
• Tranquilla River Lodge

The village of Ağva offers a secluded little piece of heaven 90 kilometres away from the city to those needing a break from Istanbul's frenetic pace. Located at the delta of the Göksu and Yeşilçay rivers on the Black Sea coast, the village of Ağva has been given the Turkish version of the Latin word 'aqua'. The banks of the rivers are occupied by several hotels offering relaxed accommodation, and more seafood restaurants than you can shake a fishing-pole at.

Although many visitors come to Ağva to be as inactive as possible, for those more inclined to heave their inert selves off the beach, fishing, swimming, canoeing and bicycle riding are all on offer. For sightseers, Kilim Koyu, Saklı Göl, and Gelin Kayası (Bride Stone) are must-sees. Gelin Kayası's claim to fame is, apparently, that it is a big white stone that resembles a bride.

And for those wishing to stay the night, Tranquilla River Lodge has eight wooden cottages that provide the necessary requirements for a comfortable stay, including king-sized beds. The fireplace at the main building is always surrounded by city escapees sipping hot red wine during winter weekends. In the summer, the crowd moves to the beach or the riverside decks for sunbathing.

Do be warned that, as with many of Turkey's coastal resorts, Ağva is closed during the off-season and an open restaurant is hard to come by. During summer weekends its hotels fill up quickly.

Polonezköy: Pole to Pole

- Leonardo
- Polka Country Hotel

Once the home of Polish refugees, this charming and peaceful village is now a popular rural retreat for Istanbulian day-trippers willing to brave the narrow windy road that leads to it. Polonezköy, offering fresh air, a sylvan setting, and myriad Polish restaurants, is located about 45 minutes from the city.

The story of Polonezköy (or Adampol) dates back to the 1840s, when Polish statesman and diplomat Adam Czartoryski, despairing of the carving up of his country by Austria, Prussia and Russia, sent a letter to the Ottoman sultan requesting a colony for his people on the outskirts of Beykoz. The subsequent arrivals (about 10 families) established a village and earned their living by dairy farming until the 1950s. To accommodate a growing number of visitors to their little village, the residents turned their farms into restaurants and bed-and-breakfasts, and Polonezköy emerged as the favoured weekend resort of today.

Leonardo, a two-storey restaurant located in the midst of the town square, offers Polish fare, as well as Turkish, French and Slavic dishes, and their weekend buffet lunch is ever-popular with visitors, as is the half-Olympic-sized swimming pool at the bottom of the garden. The recently-restored Polka Country Hotel with its 15 rooms is the best hotel in the area, and promises tranquil holidays with attentive service.

Polonezköy has been visited by several Polish dignitaries, including that most famous Pole, Karol Wojtyla, better known as the late Pope John Paul II.

A DAY AT THE BEACH

Kilyos & Bahçeköy: Surf and Sauerkraut

• Hilde Hotel & Restaurant

Located on the Black Sea coast, west of the northern mouth of the Bosphorus, the fishing village of Kilyos is the nearest retreat to Istanbul. During the summer months, it is where natives head to, beach towels tucked under their arms, in their thousands.

On the way to a day at the beach, you will pass through Bahçeköy. This small village next to the Belgrade Forest doesn't offer much apart from leafy glades and a few picnic tables, but the German gasthaus, managed by husband-and-wife team Hildegard and Yılmaz Atiker, is worth a visit for a long weekend lunch. Once sated, visitors can walk off the huge portions of schnitzel and sauerkraut in the neighbouring forest, or spend the night in one of the upstairs rooms, marked with Turkish male names instead of numbers.

Once en route to Kilyos, head to Solar Beach, which offers sunbathing during the day and a club vibe after dark, both choices accompanied by loud, thumping house music. With a bar and barbecue on the beach, and an activities programme for children, Solar Beach has something for everyone.

Should you wish to make the most of the sun on a more secluded beach, Dalia is just the ticket. Located in Demirciköy (next to Kilyos), the only noise here is the sound of waves crashing on the beach. As a bonus, there is a a good fish restaurant here, as well. A word of warning, however: the Black Sea waters are very chilly and subject to dangerous undercurrents.

contact

All telephone numbers are given for dialling locally: the country code for Turkey is 90; the city code for the European side of Istanbul is 0212; for the Asian side it is 0216. Calling from abroad, therefore, one dials (+90 212 or +90 216) plus the rest of the number given below. Telephone numbers in the retreat section are given for dialling from Istanbul. The number in brackets by the name is the page number on which the entry appears.

5. Kat [54]
Soğancı Sokak 7
Cihangir 34433 Istanbul
T   0212 293 3774
F   0212 252 3385
E   info@5kat.com
W   www.5kat.com

6:45 [110]
Kadife Sokak 21
Kadıköy 34710 Istanbul
T   0216 414 5081
F   0216 414 2750
E   bilgi@altikirkbes.com
W   www.altikirkbes.com

18 [54]
Akyol Sokak 13/A
Cihangir 34427 Istanbul
T   0212 293 2459
F   0212 293 2435

360 İstanbul [163]
İstiklal Caddesi 311/32
Beyoğlu 34430 Istanbul
T   0212 244 8192
E   misir360@hotmail.com

A La Turca [166]
Faikpaşa Yokuşu 4
Çukurcuma 34433 Istanbul
T/F 0212 245 2933

Ab'bas [99]
Cevdet Paşa Caddesi 177
Bebek 34342 Istanbul
T   0212 263 0005

Abdulla + Hamam [41]
Halıcılar Çarşısı Caddesi 53
Kapalıçarşı 34128 Istanbul
T/F 0212 522 9078
E   info@abdulla.com
W   www.abdulla.com

Accenturc [174]
Faikpaşa Yokuşu 6
Çukurcuma 34433 Istanbul
T   0212 245 7168
F   0212 245 7169
E   info@accenturc.com
W   www.accenturc.com

Adnan & Hasan [42]
Halıcılar Çarşısı Caddesi
89–90–92
Kapalıçarşı 34128 Istanbul
T   0212 527 9887
F   0212 528 0885
E   info@adnanandhasan.com
W   www.adnanandhasan.com

A'jia [122]
Kanlıca-Çubuklu Caddesi 27
Kanlıca 34805 Istanbul
T   0216 413 9300

F   0216 413 9355
E   info@ajiahotel.com
W   www.ajiahotel.com

Ali Baba Köftecisi [97]
1. Cadde 104
Arnavutköy 34345 Istanbul
T   0212 265 3612

Ali Muhiddin Hacı Bekir [38]
Hamidiye Caddesi 81–83
Bahçekapı 34112 Istanbul
T   0212 522 8543
E   hacibekir@hacibekir.com.tr
W   www.hacibekir.com.tr

Ali Usta [109]
Moda Caddesi 264/A
Moda 34710 Istanbul
T   0216 414 1880

All Sports Café [87]
Çamlık Sokak 1/2
Etiler 34337 Istanbul
T   0212 257 4299
F   0212 257 7243
E   allsports@i-gunler.com

Altı [55]
Anahtar Sokak 15
Cihangir 34433 Istanbul
T   0212 293 0849

Anemas Zindanları [47]
Dervişzade Caddesi
Ayvansaray Istanbul

Ansen 130 [124]
Meşrutiyet Caddesi 130
Tünel 34430 Istanbul
T   0212 245 8808
F   0212 245 7179
E   info@ansensuite.com
W   www.ansensuite.com

Antre Gourmet Shop [57]
Akarsu Yokuşu 52
Cihangir 34433 Istanbul
T   0212 292 8972
F   0212 244 4985
E   antre@antregourmet.com
W   www.antregourmet.com

Arab'ın Yeri [112]
İskele Caddesi 18
Salacak 34676 Istanbul
T   0216 333 3157

Armani Caffe [158]
Maçka Caddesi 35
Maçka Palas
Teşvikiye 34367 Istanbul
T   0212 224 4477
F   0212 225 1948

Art Shop [61]
Faikpaşa Yokuşu 7/2
Çukurcuma 34433 Istanbul
T 0212 245 7202
F 0212

Asitane Restaurant [140]
Kariye Camii Sokak 18
Edirnekapı 34087 Istanbul
T 0212 635 7997
F 0212 521 6631
E info@kariyeotel.com
W www.kariyeotel.com

Asri Turşucusu [58]
Ağa Hamamı Caddesi 29/A
Cihangir 34433 Istanbul
T 0212 244 4724
F 0212 249 3127

Aşşk Cafe [94]
Muallim Naci Caddesi 170/IA
Kuruçeşme 34345 Istanbul
T 0212 265 4734
F 0212 287 5705
W www.asskcafe.com

Asude Ev Yemekleri [115]
Perihan Abla Sokak 4
Kuzguncuk 34674 Istanbul
T 0216 334 4414

Atik Valide Camii [112]
Çinili Camii Sokak
Üsküdar 34664 Istanbul

Autoban [27]
Tatar Bey Sokak 1/2
Galata 34420 Istanbul
T 0212 243 8642
F 0212 243 8640
E info@autoban212.com
W www.autoban212.com

Aya Andrea [27]
Mumhane Caddesi 103
Karaköy 34425 Istanbul

Aya İlya [27]
Karanlık Fırın Sokak 6/A
Karaköy 34425 Istanbul

Aya Panteleymon [27]
Hoca Tahsin Sokak 19
Karaköy 34425 Istanbul

**Ayasofya Pansiyonları &
Konuk Evi** [34]
Soğukçeşme Sokak
Sultanahmet 34122 Istanbul
T 0212 513 3660
F 0212 513 3669
E info@ayasofyapensions.com
W www. ayasofyapensions.com

Ayça [71]
Atiye Sokak 7/8
Teşvikiye 34367 Istanbul

T 0212 219 2511
F 0212 219 2514
E ayca@aycagallery.com
W www.aycagallery.com

**AzzuR Restaurant +
BarAdox** [82]
Büyükdere Caddesi 4
Mövenpick Hotel
Levent 34330 Istanbul
T 0212 319 2929
F 0212 319 2920
E istanbul@moevenpick.com.tr
W www.moevenpick.com.tr

Babylon [21]
Şehbender Sokak 3
Tünel 34430 Istanbul
T 0212 292 7368
F 0212 243 4527
E babylon@turk.net
W www.babylon-ist.com

Bahar Pastanesi [99]
1. Cadde 46
Arnavutköy 34345 Istanbul
T 0212 265 1564

Balık Pazarı [17]
Sahne Sokak
Galatasaray Istanbul

Balıkçı Sabahattin [141]
Seyit Hasan Kuyu Sokak 50
Sultanahmet 34122 Istanbul
T 0212 458 1824

Baylan Pastanesi [155]
Muvakkithane Caddesi 19
Kadıköy 34710 Istanbul
T 0216 346 6350
F 0216 345 8879
E info@baylanpastanesi.com
W www.baylanpastanesi.com

Bebek Badem Ezmecisi [99]
Cevdet Paşa Caddesi 238/1
Bebek 34342 Istanbul
T/F 0212 263 59 84

Bebek Bar [155]
Cevdet Paşa Caddesi 34
Bebek 34342 Istanbul
T 0212 358 2000
F 0212 263 2636
E bebekhotel@bebekhotel.com.tr
W www.bebekhotel.com.tr

Bebek Kahve [100]
Cevdet Paşa Caddesi 13
Bebek 34342 Istanbul
T 0212 257 5402

Bentley Hotel [126]
Halaskargazi Caddesi 75
Harbiye 34373 Istanbul
T 0212 291 7730

F 0212 291 7740
E istanbul@bentley-hotel.com
W www.bentley-hotel.com

Beylerbeyi Sarayı [115]
Abdullahağa Caddesi
Beylerbeyi 34676 Istanbul
T 0216 321 9320
F 0216 321 9322

Beymen Nişantaşı [169]
Abdi İpekçi Caddesi 23
Nişantaşı 34367 Istanbul
T 0212 343 0404
F 0212 343 0437
W www.beymen.com.tr

Bis Wear [62]
Hayriye Sokak 20/3
Çukurcuma 34433 Istanbul
T 0212 244 7735
E bis2001@hotmail.com

Bistrott [83]
Mayadrom Alışveriş Merkezi 47/A
Akatlar 34335 Istanbul
T 0212 352 3225

**Boğaziçi Borsa
Restaurant** [149]
Lütfi Kırdar Kongre Sarayı
Harbiye 34367 Istanbul
T 0212 232 4201
F 0212 232 5856
E info@borsarestaurants.com
W www.borsarestaurants.com

Bosphorus Palace Hotel [128]
Yalıboyu Caddesi 64
Beylerbeyi 34676 Istanbul
T 0216 422 0003
F 0216 422 0012
E info@bosphoruspalace.com
W www.bosphoruspalace.com

**Bulgar Kilisesi (Sveti
Stefan)** [44]
Mürsel Paşa Caddesi 87
Balat 34087 Istanbul
T 0212 248 0921

Butik Katia [18]
Danışman Geçidi 37
Galatasaray 34430 Istanbul
T 0212 249 4605

**Büyük Saray Mozaikleri
Müzesi** [32]
Torun Sokağı, Arasta Çarşısı
Sultanahmet 34122 Istanbul
T 0212 528 4500
F 0212 512 5474

Buz Teşvikiye [161]
Abdi İpekçi Caddesi 42/2
Nişantaşı 34367 Istanbul
T 0212 291 0066

Café di Dolce [97]
Kuruçeşme Caddesi 25
Kuruçeşme 34345 Istanbul
T 0212 257 7299
F 0212 263 1305
E nilgun@cafedidolce.com
W www.cafedidolce.com

Café Marmara [18]
Taksim Meydanı
Marmara Istanbul Hotel
Taksim 34437 Istanbul
T 0212 251 4696
F 0212 244 0509
W www.cafemarmara.com

Café Zanzibar [145]
Cemil Topuzlu Caddesi 112
Caddebostan 34728 Istanbul
T 0216 385 6059
F 0216 369 8516
E zanzibarkosk@superonline.
   com

Cağaloğlu Hamamı [36]
Kazım İsmail Gürkan Caddesi 34
Cağaloğlu 34110 Istanbul
T 0212 522 2424
F 0212 512 8553
E info@cagagluhamami.com.tr
W www.cagagluhamami.com.tr

Carne [94]
Muallim Naci Caddesi 17A
Ortaköy 34347 Istanbul
T 0212 259 1280
F 0212 259 1282
E carne@carne.com.tr
W www.carne.com.tr

Çemberlitaş Hamamı [35]
Vezirhanı Caddesi 8
Çemberlitaş 34120 Istanbul
T 0212 522 7974
F 0212 511 2535
E contact@cemberlitashamami.
   com.tr
W www.cemberlitashamami.
   com.tr

Cemilzade [109]
Cemil Topuzlu Caddesi 7/4
Kadıköy 34726 Istanbul
T 0216 385 0423
F 0216 385 5189
E cemilzade@cemilzade.com.tr
W www.cemilzade.com.tr

Ceremony [75]
Ayazmadere Sokak 30/1
Dikilitaş 34349 Istanbul
T 0212 216 4595
F 0212 216 9628
E ceremony@superonline.com

Changa [142]
Sıraselviler Caddesi 87/1
Taksim 34433 Istanbul
T 0212 249 1348

F 0212 249 1157
E sata@tnn.net
W www.changa-istanbul.com

Cibalikapı Balıkçısı [44]
Abdülezel Paşa Caddesi 7
Cibali 34750 Istanbul
T 0212 533 2846
F 0212 533 2789
E admin@cibalikapibalikcisi.com
W www.cibalikapibalikcisi.com

City Farm [84]
Mayadrom Alışveriş Merkezi 29
Akatlar 34335 Istanbul
T 0212 351 53 75
F 0212 351 53 65
E cityfarm@cityfarm.com.tr

Çiya [112]
Güneşli Bahçe Sokak 43-44-48/B
Caferağa Mahallesi
Kadıköy 34710 Istanbul
T 0216 336 3013
F 0216 349 1902
E info@ciya.com.tr
W www.ciya.com.tr

Cook Book [76]
Güzelbahçe Sokak 5/2
Nişantaşı 34365 Istanbul
T 0212 219 1394
F 0212 219 1395
E info@cookbook-nisantasi.com
W www.cookbook-nisantasi.com

Da Mario [85]
Dil Hayat Sokak 7
Etiler 34337 Istanbul
T 0212 265 1596
E damario@istanbuldoors.com
W www.istanbuldoors.com

Dank! [87]
Mayadrom Uptown Alışveriş
Merkezi
P2 Garaj Katı
Etiler 34100 Istanbul
T 0212 352 6044
F 0212 352 6046
E info@dank-design.com
W www.dank-design.com

Darüzziyafe [145]
Şifahane Sokak 6
Süleymaniye 34134 Istanbul
T 0212 511 8414
F 0212 526 1891
E daruzziyafe@daruzziyafe.com
W www.daruzziyafe.com

Deli Kızın Yeri [43]
Halıcılar Çarşısı Caddesi 42
Kapalıçarşı 34128 Istanbul
T/F 0212 511 1914
E crazylady@garlin.com
W www.delikiz.com

Deniz Tunç Design [75]
Güzelbahçe Sokak 5/1
Nişantaşı 34365 Istanbul
T 0212 232 1216
F 0212 246 4826

Derin Design [70]
Abdi İpekçi Caddesi 77/1
Maçka 34365 Istanbul
T 0212 225 2003
F 0212 225 1955
E info@derindesign.com
W www.derindesign.com

Derishow [173]
Yeşilçimen Sokak 17
Fulya 34353 Istanbul
T 0212 259 7255
F 0212 259 7259
E derishow@tnn.net

Dilara'sabra Cadabra [62]
Fransız Sokağı 6
Galatasaray 34433 Istanbul
T 0212 244 4745
E sabracadabra@e-kolay.net

Dilmen Kitabevi [43]
Sahaflar Çarşısı Sokak 20
Beyazıt 34450 Istanbul
T 0212 527 9934
F 0212 426 8454

Doğa Balık [57]
Akarsu Yokuşu 46
Hotel Zurich
Cihangir 34433 Istanbul
T 0212 293 9144
F 0212 293 9143
E dogabalik@doga-balik.com
W www.doga-balik.com

Dört Mevsim [82]
Mayadrom Alışveriş Merkezi 34
Akatlar 34335 Istanbul
T 0212 352 2689
F 0212 352 2691
E dortmevsim@dortmevsim.com
W www.dortmevsim.com

Ece Aynalı Meyhane [94]
Tramvay Caddesi 104
Kuruçeşme 34345 Istanbul
T 0212 265 9600
F 0212 265 9620

**Ela Cindoruk –
Nazan Pak** [72]
Atiye Sokak 14
Teşvikiye 34365 Istanbul
T 0212 232 2664
F 0212 241 5419

Elaidi [73]
Teşvikiye Caddesi 129/1
Teşvikiye 34365 Istanbul
T 0212 231 0508

F 0212 230 3599
E info@elaidi.net
W www.elaidi.net

Emek 2 Kahve [103]
Köybaşı Caddesi Daire Sokak
Yeniköy Istanbul
T 0212 223 7728
F 0212 262 3231

Emirgan Korusu [102]
Emirgan Korusu Caddesi
Emirgan Istanbul

Erenler Nargile [42]
Çorlulu Ali Paşa Medresesi 36/28
Beyazıt 34126 Istanbul
T 0212 511 8853

Erol Kundura [174]
Rumeli Caddesi 21-23
Nişantaşı 34367 Istanbul
T 0212 233 8613
E quartos@e-kolay.net

Eşik Design [62]
Hayriye Sokak 20/2
Galatasaray 34443 Istanbul
T 0212 244 4987
F 0212 251 8088
E info@esik.org
W www.esik.org

Ethemefendi 36 [109]
Ethemefendi Caddesi 36
Erenköy 34738 Istanbul
T 0216 385 4131
F 0216 356 5989
E info@ethemefendi36.com
W www.ethemefendi36.com

Ev+ [76]
Ihlamur Nişantaşı Yolu 9/3
Nişantaşı 34365 Istanbul
T 0212 232 1758
F 0212 231 4933

Evihan [58]
Altıpatlar Sokak 8
Çukurcuma 34433 Istanbul
T 0212 244 0034
F 0212 244 0035
E info@evihan.com
W www.evihan.com

Fatih Karadeniz Pidecisi [44]
Büyük Karaman Caddesi 57
Fatih 34083 Istanbul
T 0212 523 9795

Feriye Lokantası [144]
Çırağan Caddesi 124
Ortaköy Istanbul
T 0212 227 2216
F 0212 236 5799
E feriye@feriye.com
W www.feriye.com

Fes Café [41]
Halıcılar Çarşısı Caddesi 62
Kapalıçarşı 34128 Istanbul
T 0212 528 1613
F 0212 522 9078

Foodie [87]
Güzel Konutlar Sitesi 1-2
Ulus 34340 Istanbul
T 0212 287 4521
F 0212 287 4520

Galata Evi [24]
Galata Kulesi Sokak 61
Galata 34420 Istanbul
T/F 0212 245 1861
E galata61@hotmail.com
W www.thegalatahouse.com

Galata Kulesi [24]
Galata Kulesi Sokak
Galata 34420 Istanbul
T 0212 293 8180
F 0212 245 2133
E info@galatatower.net
W www.galatatower.net

Galata Mevlevihanesi [24]
Galip Dede Caddesi 15
Tünel 34430 Istanbul
T 0212 245 4141
F 0212 243 5045

Galerist [18]
İstiklal Caddesi 311/4
Beyoğlu 34430 Istanbul
T 0212 244 8230
F 0212 244 8229
E info@galerist.com.tr
W www.galerist.com.tr

Gerekli Şeyler [75]
Kalıpçı Sokak 111/1
Teşvikiye 34365 Istanbul
T 0212 291 0689
F 0212 291 0675

GES [87]
Esra Sokak G3 Blok D/2
Etiler 34340 Istanbul
T 0212 257 3169
F 0212 257 1708
E info@gescollection.com
W www.gescollection.com

Gilan [87]
Akmerkez Alışveriş Merkezi 123
Etiler 34337 Istanbul
T 0212 282 0576
F 0212 282 0579
E info@gilan.com.tr
W www.gilan.com.tr

Giritli [32]
Keresteci Hakkı Sokak
Cankurtaran 34122 Istanbul
T 0212 458 2270

F 0212 518 5060
E giritli_ist@giritlirestoran.com
W www.giritlirestoran.com

Gönül Paksoy [170]
Atiye Sokak 1/3 and 6/A
Teşvikiye 34365 Istanbul
T 0212 236 0209
Atiye Sokak 6/A
Teşvikiye 34365 Istanbul
T 0212 261 9081

Grand Hotel De Londres [18]
Meşrutiyet Caddesi 117
Tepebaşı 34420 Istanbul
T 0212 293 1619
F 0212 245 0671
E londra@londrahotel.net
W www.londrahotel.net

Güneş Halı [70]
Mim Kemal Öke Caddesi 5
Nişantaşı 34365 Istanbul
T 0212 225 1968
F 0212 225 1940

Hacı Abdullah [150]
Sakızağacı Caddesi 17
Beyoğlu 34440 Istanbul
T 0212 293 8561
F 0212 244 32 97
E haciabdullah@haciabdullah.com.tr
W www.haciabdullah.com.tr

Halide d. [58]
Turnacıbaşı Sokak 71/1
Çukurcuma 34433 Istanbul
T 0212 245 7775
F 0212 245 7774
W www.halided.com

Hamdi Et Lokantası [39]
Kalçın Sokak 17
Eminönü 34116 Istanbul
T 0212 528 0390
F 0212 528 4991
E info@hamdirestorant.com.tr
W www.hamdirestorant.com.tr

Harbiye Askeri Müzesi [68]
Valikonağı Caddesi
Harbiye 34367 Istanbul
T 0212 233 2720
F 0212 2968618

Harvard Cafe [84]
Seher Yıldızı Sokak 6
Etiler 34337 Istanbul
T/F 0212 287 1051
E harvardcafe@harvardcafe.com.tr
W www.harvardcafe.com.tr

Havai Lostra Salonu [16]
Sakızağacı Caddesi 27/1
Beyoğlu 34440 Istanbul
T 0212 245 1652

Hayal Kahvesi [115]
Burunbahçe Mevkii
Kanlıca Istanbul

Haydarpaşa Tren İstasyonu [112]
İstasyon Caddesi
Rasimpaşa 34714 Istanbul
T 0216 348 8020

Hıdiv Kasrı [116]
Çubuklu Hıdiv Yolu 32
Beykoz 34805 Istanbul
T 0216 413 9644
F 0216 413 96 99
E info@beltur.com
W www.beltur.com.tr

Hotel Daphnis [130]
Sadrazam Ali Paşa Caddesi 26
Fener 34220 Istanbul
T 0212 531 4858
F 0212 532 8992
E info@hoteldaphnis.com
W www.hoteldaphnis.com

Hotel Empress Zoe [132]
Adliye Sokak 10
Sultanahmet 34112 Istanbul
T 0212 518 2504
F 0212 518 5699
E info@emzoe.com
W www.emzoe.com

The House Cafe [149]
Atiye Sokak 10/1
Teşvikiye 34365 Istanbul
T/F 0212 259 2377

Hünkar [68]
Mim Kemal Öke Caddesi 21
Nişantaşı 34367 Istanbul
T 0212 225 4665
F 0212 291 7292

İbrahim Paşa Hotel [134]
Terzihane Sokak 5
Sultanahmet 34122 Istanbul
T 0212 518 0394
F 0212 518 4457
E contact@ibrahimpasha.com
W www.ibrahimpasha.com

Ihlamur Kasrı [76]
Ihlamur Nişantaşı Yolu
Beşiktaş 34353 Istanbul
T 0212 259 5086

İnci Pastanesi [17]
İstiklal Caddesi 124/2
Beyoğlu 34430 Istanbul
T 0212 243 2412

İskele [102]
İskele Meydanı 4/1
Rumelihisarı 34450 Istanbul
T 0212 263 2997
F 0212 263 4064

E info@iskelebalik.com
W www.iskelebalik.com

İstanbul Arkeoloji Müzeleri [36]
Osman Hamdi Bey Yokuşu
Sultanahmet 34122 Istanbul
T 0212 520 7740
F 0212 527 4300

İstanbul Modern Museum + Café [27 and 160]
Meclis-i Mebusan Caddesi
Antrepo 4
Karaköy 34425 Istanbul
T 0212 243 4318
F 0212 243 4319
E info@istanbulmodern.org
W www.istanbulmodern.org

İstiridye Balık Lokantası [27]
Mumhane Caddesi 94
Karaköy 34425 Istanbul
T 0212 249 1772

İznik Foundation [175]
Öksüz Çocuk Sokak 7
Kuruçeşme 34345 Istanbul
T 0212 287 3243
F 0212 287 3247
E info@iznik.com
W www.iznik.com

Kafe Ara [18]
Tosbağa Sokak 8
Galatasaray 34430 Istanbul
T 0212 245 4105
F 0212 245 4104
E info@arakafe.com

Kaffeehaus [24]
Tünel Meydanı 4
Tünel 34430 Istanbul
T 0212 245 4028
F 0212 245 4029
W www.kaffeehaus-istanbul.com

Kalsedon Maden İşletmeleri [35]
Caferiye Sokak 2
Sultanahmet 34122 Istanbul
T 0212 513 4570
F 0212 512 2120
E sirrigercin@superonline.com
W www.kalsedon.com.tr

Kanaat Lokantası [148]
Selmani Pak Caddesi 25
Üsküdar 34664 Istanbul
T 0216 553 3791
F 0216 341 6855

Kantin [75]
Akkavak Sokak 16/2
Nişantaşı 34365 Istanbul
T 0212 219 3114
F 0212 219 2807

Karaköy Güllüoğlu Baklavacısı [27]
Mumhane Caddesi 171
Karaköy 34425 Istanbul
T 0212 243 1376
F 0212 249 9767
E info@gulluoglu.biz
W www.gulluoglu.biz

Karga(rt) [110]
Kadife Sokak 16
Kadıköy 81300 Istanbul
T 0216 330 3151
F 0216 346 5546
E info@kargart.org
W www.kargart.org

Karışma Sen [32]
Kennedy Caddesi 30
Ahırkapı 34122 Istanbul
T 0212 517 6892
E ahmet@teoman.net

Kay's [54]
Güneşli Sokak 32
Cihangir 34433 Istanbul
T 0212 249 5024

Kiliza [84]
4. Gazeteciler Sitesi A 28/2
Levent 34335 Istanbul
T 0212 325 7170
F 0212 325 5542
W www.kiliza.com

Kıyı [140]
Kefeliköy Caddesi 126
Tarabya 34457 Istanbul
T 0212 262 0002
F 0212 262 0244
E info@kiyi.com.tr
W www.kiyi.com.tr

Koç Deri [39]
Kürkçüler Caddesi 22–46
Kapalıçarşı 34120 Istanbul
T 0212 527 5553
F 0212 527 8677
E info@kocderi.com
W www.kocderi.com

Koço Restaurant [109]
Moda Caddesi 265
Kadıköy 34710 Istanbul
T 0216 336 0795
F 0216 337 7044

Köfteci Arnavut [46]
Mürsel Paşa Caddesi 155
Balat 34087 Istanbul
T 0212 531 6652

Konak Pastanesi [73]
Valikonağı Caddesi 34/1
Nişantaşı 34365 Istanbul
T 0212 225 2872

Koyu Kahve [61]
Hayriye Sokak 5/2–3
Galatasaray 34430 Istanbul
T   0212 251 7714

Küçük Ayasofya Camii [32]
Küçük Ayasofya Caddesi
Cankurtaran 34122 Istanbul

Küçüksu Kasrı [115]
Küçüksu Çayırı Sahili
Anadolu Hisarı 34815 Istanbul
T   0216 332 02 37

La Cave [57]
Sıraselviler Caddesi 207
Çağdaş Market 2nd Floor
Cihangir 34433 Istanbul
T   0212 243 2405
F   0212 243 5156
E   lacave@superonline.com
W www.lacavesarap.com

La Maison [146]
Müvezzi Caddesi 63
Beşiktaş 34349 Istanbul
T   0212 227 4263
F   0212 227 4278
E   mail@lamaison.com.tr
W www.lamaison.com.tr

Lacivert [116]
Körfez Caddesi 57/A
Anadolu Hisarı 34810 Istanbul
T   0216 413 4224
F   0216 425 1974
E   info@lacivertrestaurant.com
W www.lacivertrestaurant.com

Lale Plak [23]
Galip Dede Caddesi 1
Tünel 34420 Istanbul
T   0212 293 7739
F   0212 243 6615
E   laleplak@tnn.net

Laleli Zeytinyağları [100]
Cevdet Paşa Caddesi 97/A
Bebek 34342 Istanbul
T/F 0212 265 6617
E   taylieli@duzen.com.tr
W www.zeytinim.com.tr

Leb-i Derya [154]
Kumbaracı Yokuşu 115
Beyoğlu 34433 Istanbul
T   0212 293 4989
F   0212 243 9556
E   info@lebiderya.com
W www.lebiderya.com

Leyla [57]
Akarsu Yokuşu 46
Cihangir 34433 Istanbul
T   0212 244 5350
F   0212 244 5335
E   leyla@leyla2004.com
W www.leyla2004.com

Loft [68]
Lütfi Kırdar Kongre Sarayı
Harbiye 34367 Istanbul
T 0212 219 6384
F   0212 232 5856
E info@borsarestaurants.com
W www.loftrestbar.com

Lokal [20]
Müeyyet Sokak 9
Tünel 34430 Istanbul
T   0212 245 5743
F   0212 245 5744
E   info@lokal-istanbul.com
W www.lokal-istanbul.com

Lokanta [141]
Meşrutiyet Caddesi 149/1
Tepebaşı 34430 Istanbul
T   0212 245 6070
F   0212 245 6039
E   lokanta@istanbulyi.com
W www.istanbulyi.com

L'Orient [167]
Şerif Ağa Sokak 22–23
İçbedesten Kapalıçarşı 34128
Istanbul
T/F 0212 520 7046
E   murat-bilir@usa.net
W www.muratbilir.com

Lucca [99]
Cevdet Paşa Caddesi 51/B
Bebek 34342 Istanbul
T   0212 257 1255
F   0212 257 1266

Mangerie [99]
Cevdet Paşa Caddesi 69/3
Bebek 34342 Istanbul
T   0212 263 51 99
E   eliftopkaya@superonline.com
W www.mangerie.com.tr

**Meşhur Kireçburnu
Fırını** [103]
Kireçburnu Caddesi 21
Kireçburnu 34457 Istanbul
T   0212 262 1059
F   0212 262 5403

Mihrimah Sultan Camii [47]
Hocaçakır Caddesi
Edirnekapı 34091 Istanbul

**Milli Reasürans Sanat
Galerisi** [70]
Teşvikiye Caddesi 43–57
Teşvikiye 34365 Istanbul
T   0212 230 1976
F   0212 219 6258
E   info@millireasuranssanat
    galerisi.com
W www.millireasuranssanat
    galerisi.com

Mimkemal 19 [148]
Mim Kemal Öke Caddesi 19
Nişantaşı 34367 Istanbul
T   0212 224 1987
F   0212 224 3587
E   semsa@mimkemal19.com
W www.mimkemal19.com

Mine Kerse [61]
Faikpaşa Yokuşu 1/A
Çukurcuma 34425 Istanbul
T   0212 243 0047
F   0212 251 8674
E   minekerse@minartekstil.com

Mısır Çarşısı [167]
Mısır Çarşısı
Eminönü 34116 Istanbul

Miss Pizza [55]
Havyar Sokak 7
Cihangir 34433 Istanbul
T   0212 251 3278

Moda Teras [109]
Moda Mektebi Sokak 7/9
Moda 34752 Istanbul
T   0216 338 7040
E   info@modateras.com
W www.modateras.com

Nardis Jazz Club [24]
Kuledibi Sokak 14
Galata 34420 Istanbul
T   0212 244 6327
F   0212 244 6328
E   focan@nardisjazz.com
W www.nardisjazz.com

NuPera + NuTeras [160]
Meşrutiyet Caddesi 149
Tepebaşı 34430 Istanbul
T   0212 245 6070
E   nupera@marsconcept.com
W www.marsconcept.com

Ottoman Empire [75]
Şakayık Sokak 59/1
Teşvikiye 34365 Istanbul
T   0212 296 5619
F   0212 296 0823
W www.ottomanempiretshirts.
    com

**Panaghia Mouchliotissa
(Moğolların Meryemi)** [46]
Sadrazam Ali Paşa Caddesi
Balat 34087 Istanbul

Pandeli [151]
Mısır Çarşısı 1
Eminönü 34116 Istanbul
T   0212 527 3909
F   0212 522 5534

Pando [156]
Mumcu Sokak 5
Beşiktaş 34353 Istanbul
T   0212 258 2616

Paper Moon [147]
Ahmet Adnan Saygun Caddesi
Ulus 34337 Istanbul
T   0212 282 1616
F   0212 282 1334

Park Şamdan [144]
Mim Kemal Öke Caddesi 18
Nişantaşı 34367 Istanbul
T   0212 225 07 10
F   0212 225 3695

Paşabahçe [172]
Teşvikiye Caddesi 117
Teşvikiye 34365 Istanbul
T   0212 233 50 05
E   magaza@sisecam.com.tr
W www.pasabahce.com.tr

Patisserie Markiz [157]
İstiklal Caddesi 360
Beyoğlu 34430 Istanbul
T   0212 251 7581
F   0212 251 7582
E   info@passagemarkiz.com
W www.markiz.com

**Pera Palas + Orient
Bar** [136 and 157]
Meşrutiyet Caddesi 98–100
Tepebaşı 34430 Istanbul
T   0212 251 4560
F   0212 251 4089
E   perapalas@perapalas.com
W www.perapalas.com

Pera Thai [22]
Meşrutiyet Caddesi 134
Tünel 34430 Istanbul
T   0212 245 5725
F   0212 245 5726
E   info@perathai.com
W www.perathai.com

PG Art Gallery [99]
Cevdet Paşa Caddesi 386/2–3
Bebek 34342 Istanbul
T   0212 263 3390
F   0212 263 3724

Pied de Poule [61]
Faikpaşa Yokuşu 19/1
Çukurcuma 34425 Istanbul
T   0212 245 8116

Pierre Loti Café [154]
Gümüşsuyu Balmumcu Sokak 1
Eyüp 34050 Istanbul
T   0212 581 2696

Proje 4L [83]
Harman Sokak
Harmancı Giz Plaza
Levent 34330 Istanbul
T   0212 281 5150
F   0212 283 1739
E   info@proje4l.org
W www.proje4l.org

Rahmi M Koç Müzesi [48]
Hasköy Caddesi 27
Hasköy 34445 Istanbul
T 0212 297 6639
F 0212 297 6637
E rmkmuseum@koc.com.tr
W www.rmk-museum.org.tr

Rakıcı [23]
Sofyalı Sokak 5/1
Tünel 34430 Istanbul
T/F 0212 249 6979
E rakici@rakiciasmalimescit.com
W www.rakiciasmalimescit.com

Refik [23]
Sofyalı Sokak 7
Tünel 34430 Istanbul
T 0212 245 7879
F 0212 243 2834

Robinson Crusoe Kitabevi
[20]
İstiklal Caddesi 389
Beyoğlu 34433 Istanbul
T 0212 293 6968
F 0212 251 1735
E rob@tnn.net

Sade Kahve [102]
Yahya Kemal Caddesi 36
Rumelihisarı 34342 Istanbul
T/F 0212 358 2324
E info@sadekahve.com
W www.sadekahve.com

Safa Meyhanesi [158]
İmrahor İlyas Bey Caddesi 169
Yedikule 34109 Istanbul
T 0212 585 5594

Sakıp Sabancı Müzesi [100]
İstinye Caddesi 22
Emirgan 34460 Istanbul
T 0212 277 2200
F 0212 229 4914
E muze@sabanciuniv.edu
W muze.sabanciuniv.edu

Sarnıç Restaurant [34]
Soğukçeşme Sokak
Sultanahmet 34122 Istanbul
T 0212 513 3660
F 0212 513 3669

Savoy Pastanesi [58]
Sıraselviler Caddesi 181–83A
Cihangir 34433 Istanbul
T 0212 249 1818
F 0212 293 4670
E info@savoypastanesi.com
W www.savoypastanesi.com

Şayan 24 [88]
Nispetiye Caddesi Petrol Sitesi 2
Etiler 34337 Istanbul
T 0212 270 2947

Sedir [94]
Mecidiye Köprüsü Sokak 16–18
Ortaköy 34347 Istanbul
T 0212 327 9870
F 0212 327 9347
E info@sediristanbul.com

Sefahathane [162]
Atlas Pasajı Girişi
Beyoğlu 34430 Istanbul
T 0212 251 2245

Şimdi [21]
Asmalı Mescit Sokak 8
Tünel 34430 Istanbul
T 0212 252 5443

Sirkeci Tren Garı [38]
İstasyon Caddesi 24/2
Sirkeci 34110 Istanbul
T 0212 511 5888

Sofyalı [23]
Sofyalı Sokak 9
Tünel 34430 Istanbul
T 0212 245 0362

**Sokullu Mehmet
Paşa Camii** [32]
Şehit Mehmet Paşa Sokak 20
Sultanahmet 34122 Istanbul

Stoa [172]
Hayriye Sokak 18/1
Galatasaray 34425 Istanbul
T/F 0212 251 4098
E stoa@tardukuman.com
W www.tardukuman.com

Süleymaniye Camii [44]
Prof. Sıddık Sami Onar Caddesi
Süleymaniye Istanbul

Suna'nın Yeri [115]
İskele Caddesi 4
Kandilli 34684 Istanbul
T 0216 332 3241

Sunset Grill & Bar [88]
Yol Sokak 2
Ulus 34340 Istanbul
T 0212 287 0357
E sunsetgrill@superonline.com

Süreyya Sineması [112]
Bahariye Caddesi 29
Kadıköy 34713 Istanbul
T 0216 336 0682
F 0216 346 5811
E yorum@sureyya.com
W www.sureyya.com

Şütte [87]
Nispetiye Caddesi 52
Etiler 34337 Istanbul
T 0212 263 6656

Suzanne Simon [61]
Faikpaşa Yokuşu 1
Çukurcuma Istanbul
T 0212 244 9663
E suzanne@simontekstil.com

Symrna [57]
Akarsu Yokuşu 29
Cihangir 34433 Istanbul
T 0212 244 2466

Symrna Patisserie [57]
Yeni Yuva Sokak 2/1
Cihangir 34433 Istanbul
T 0212 244 4838

Tarihi Haliç İşkembecisi [46]
Abdülezel Paşa Caddesi 315
Fener 34083 Istanbul
T 0212 534 94 14
F 0212 621 8518

Touchdown [71]
Milli Reasürans Çarşısı 61/11
Teşvikiye 34367 Istanbul
T 0212 231 3671
E info@touchdown.com.tr
W www.touchdown.com.tr

Tünel [22]
Tünel Meydanı
İstiklal Caddesi
Tünel Istanbul

**Türk ve İslam Eserleri
Müzesi** [34]
Atmeydanı Sokağı 46
Sultanahmet 34122 Istanbul
T 0212 518 1805
F 0212 518 1807
E tiemist@superonline.com
W www.tiem.org

Ulus 29 + Club 29 [143]
Ahmet Adnan Saygun Caddesi
Ulus 34340 Istanbul
T 0212 358 2929
F 0212 265 2242
E ulus29@club29.com
W www.club29.com

Ümit Ünal [168]
Ensiz Sokak 3
Asmalı Mescit Mahallesi
Tünel 34430 Istanbul
T 0212 245 7886
F 0212 249 3239
E umitunal@umitunal.com
W www.umitunal.com

Urart [72]
Abdi İpekçi Caddesi 18/1
Nişantaşı 34367 Istanbul
T 0212 246 7194
E info@urart.com.tr
W www.urart.com.tr

Üsküdar Bitpazarı [112]
Büyükhamam Sokak
Üsküdar Istanbul

**Vakko Beyoğlu – Home
Décor** [16]
İstiklal Caddesi 123–125, 2nd Floor
Beyoğlu 34430 Istanbul
T 0212 251 4092
F 0212 245 4099
E beyoglu@vakko.com.tr
W www.vakko.com.tr

Vefa Bozacısı [156]
Katip Çelebi Caddesi 104/1
Vefa 34470 Istanbul
T 0212 519 4922
F 0212 512 9054
E vefa@vefa.com.tr
W www.vefa.com.tr

Viktor Levi [161]
Hamalbaşı Caddesi 12
Galatasaray 34435 Istanbul
T 0212 249 6085
F 0212 249 6275
E info@viktorlevi.com
W www.viktorlevi.com

Vogue [159]
Süleyman Seber Caddesi
BJK Plaza 92, 13th Floor
Beşiktaş 34357 Istanbul
T 0212 227 2545
E vogue@istanbuldoors.com
W www.istanbuldoors.com

Yakup 2 [159]
Asmalı Mescit Sokak 35–37
Tünel 34430 Istanbul
T 0212 249 2925
F 0212 251 3181

Yanyalı Fehmi Lokantası [110]
Yağlıkçı İsmail Sokak 1
Kadıköy 34714 Istanbul
T 0216 336 3333

Yedi Sekiz Hasan Paşa [97]
Şehit Asım Caddesi 12
Beşiktaş 34353 Istanbul
T 0212 261 9766

Yıldız Şale [94]
Palanga Caddesi 23
Yıldız Parkı
Beşiktaş Istanbul

Yuşa Tepesi [116]
Yuşa Tepesi Yolu
Ortaçeşme Istanbul

Zaman Tüneli [58]
Turnacıbaşı Sokak 80
Çukurcuma 34433 Istanbul

Zeynel [103]
Köybaşı Caddesi 144
Yeniköy 34464 Istanbul
T 0212 262 8987
E info@zeynel.com.tr
W www.zeynel.com.tr

Zeynep Erol [171]
Atiye Sokak 8/3
Nişantaşı 34367 Istanbul
T 0212 236 4668
F 0212 261 8177
E zeynep@zeyneperol.com
W www.zeyneperol.com

Zeyrek Camii [44]
İbadethane Arkası Sokak
Fatih 34083 Istanbul

Zeyrekhane [44]
İbadethane Arkası Sokak 10
Fatih 34083 Istanbul
T 0212 532 2778
F 0212 532 2747

THE PRINCES' ISLANDS [178]

Seabuses depart from the
Bostancı (Asian side) or Kabataş
(European side) quays every 2
hours in the summer (every 1 hour
at peak hours). Or take the vapur
(ferry) from Bostancı or Sirkeci;
the journey takes approximately 1
hour.

Splendid Palace Hotel
23 Nisan Caddesi 53
Büyükada 34970 Istanbul
T 0216 382 6951
Rooms from €60

Milto
İskele Yanı Büyükada
Büyükada 34970 Istanbul
T 0216 382 5312

Halki Palace Hotel
Refah Şehitleri Caddesi 88
Heybeliada 34973 Istanbul
T 0216 351 0025
F 0216 351 8483
E halki.palace@ibm.net
W www.merithotels.com
Rooms from €70

AĞVA [180]

By car, take the Ümraniye-Şile
route to Şile. After passing Şile,
take the seaside road to Ağva. The
journey is approximately 1 hour 30
minutes. Buses leave from
Üsküdar to Şile-Ağva every hour.

Tranquilla River Lodge
Kurfalı Köyü Göksu Deresi Kıyısı
Ağva 34991 Istanbul
T 0216 721 7377
E info@tranquilla.com.tr
W www.tranquilla.com.tr

POLONEZKÖY [182]

By car, drive through Kavacık and
turn left after about 1 km. Or take
the Ümraniye Sarıgazı exit off the
TEM Highway, taking the road to
Cumhuriyet Village, and turning
left upon reaching the village.
Alternatively, drive from Beykoz to
Mahmut Şevket Paşa, and from
there to Üçpınarlar, and turn
south. There is no public
transportation to and from
Polonezköy.

Polka Country Hotel
Cumhuriyet Yolu 36
Polonezköy 34829 Istanbul
T 0216 432 3220
F 0216 432 3221
E info@polkahotel.com
W www.polkahotel.com

Leonardo
Köyiçi Sokak 32
Polonezköy 34829 Istanbul

T 0216 432 3082
F 0216 432 3054
E info@leonardorestaurant.com
W www.leonardorestaurant.com

KILYOS & BAHÇEKÖY [184]

By car, drive through Sarıyer and
then take the seaside road. In the
summer there is a great deal of
traffic on this road. An alternative
is to take the road from Maslak to
Sarıyer, following the signs to
Kilyos. En route you will pass
through Bahçeköy. The journey
takes approximately 45 minutes.
Buses also run from Sarıyer to
Kilyos.

Hilde
Hunca Caddesi 6
Bahçeköy Istanbul
T/F 0212 226 1202

Solar Beach Club
Kilya Resort Otel Turban Yolu 4
Kilyos Istanbul
T 0212 201 1012
F 0212 201 2422
E info@solar-beach.com
W www.solar-beach.com

Dalia Beach Club
Demirciköy
T 0212 2040368